SONGS OF THE SEA
AND
SAILORS' CHANTEYS

SONGS OF THE SEA & SAILORS' CHANTEYS : AN ANTHOLOGY ❄ SELECTED AND ARRANGED BY ROBERT FROTHINGHAM

Granger Index Reprint Series

BOOKS FOR LIBRARIES PRESS
FREEPORT, NEW YORK

STANDARD BOOK NUMBER:
8369-6103-X

LIBRARY OF CONGRESS CATALOG CARD NUMBER:
70-99029

MANUFACTURED
BY
HALLMARK LITHOGRAPHERS, INC.
IN THE U.S.A.

FOREWORD

Most tolerant and patient reader —

    "What's in a name?"

IN connection with this query, let me suggest that you do not run your curious eye down the list of authors herein represented with the expectation of finding many celebrities. Famous poets and such poetry as suits you and me do not always travel hand in hand. If, however, you will take the time for a leisurely voyage through the little book itself, you'll be both surprised and well repaid to note the great variety of beautiful and virile sea-verse that has been written by a goodly number of latter-day and mightily worth-while poets, some of whose lights, comparatively speaking, have been hidden under a bushel.

Barring the immortal verse of an exceeding few who flourished prior to and during the Victorian era, very little sea-poetry worthy the name was written previous to the advent of Kipling — a bare thirty years ago. Take the human note out of poetry, no matter how faultless its technique, and we have left something closely resembling "sounding brass and tinkling cymbal," which leads me to say that this compilation includes only such material as carries with it a definite human interest. To be the lucky delver who brings such an array of dynamic verse before an ever-widening range of readers is a joy reserved for the anthologist alone.

It is a most interesting fact that with two notable exceptions practically all the worth-while poetry dealing with the sea has been written by landsmen. These exceptions are John Masefield, the versatile Briton who has come into his own, and Bill Adams, of California, who, close to the half-century mark, is just "arriving." Both of these men served before the mast in their youth, when the full-rigged ship was Empress of the High Seas, and to their dying day will never get the tang of salt-water out of their nostrils. There is a poignancy to much of Adams's verse which reveals his Celtic ancestry and takes swift toll of a man's emotions. Though he will never sail the seas again, he will always be under the spell of a glowing love for a ship and the "fenceless meadows," and he paints Jack afloat and ashore as no other salt-water poet has ever visioned him.

Another popular British sea-poet whose rhyme would indicate a long apprenticeship in the fo'c'sle and an intimate acquaintance with London's famous docks on Thames-side, is C. Fox Smith. It is known to comparatively few that the initial "C" is an abbreviation of Cicely, and that this much-admired and trenchant versifier is a woman who, had she been born a man, would, doubtless, be a British Admiral of the Fleet by this time.

* * * *

It is eminently fitting that the Sailors' Chanteys — eloquent of a day that is past never to return — should be recorded here with the music to which they were sung a hundred years ago. Not a harbor in either the eastern or the western hemisphere but has rung to these ancient airs. They have broken the silences of tropic seas and mingled with the howl of the tempest off Cape Horn. Such melodies can never die, ghosts though they be of a bygone day. The old-time "able seaman" sang as he worked, and it is significant of the fearful hardships of those early days that there was at least one chantey exclusively devoted to his opinion of a brutal ship-master, generally sung while dropping the anchor on return to port after a long voyage: "Leave her, Johnny, leave her." The singing of that chantey at such a time was the sailorman's method of serving notice on a skipper shorn of further retaliation that he would have to find a new crew for the next voyage.

Ah! those were the good old days, in comparison with which the roar of a chantey on the fo'c'sle of an ocean greyhound or a tramp steamship to-day would be like a foreign language to the great majority of the sailors assembled, not to mention that famous old "fore-bitter," "Farewell and adieu to you, fair Spanish ladies," which was a prime favorite nearly two hundred years agone, and will never be heard again on the deck of any ship — "Sic transit gloria!"

What's that? You don't know what a "fore-bitter" is? Well — I had to look it up myself and am glad to pass it on to you. In contradistinction to the chanteys, which were always sung by the ship's crew in chorus, led by the chantey-man, either at the capstan while raising the anchor or hauling on the halyards — work confined exclusively to merchant ships — the fore-bitter was a sentimental ballad, sung for entertainment only, on British naval vessels where the chantey was never permitted, as all work aboard warships was done in silence. The singer was chosen, first for his good memory, as the songs were always of great length and never written, and second for his vocal power. He always stood on the fore-bitts, a timber construction near the foremast, raised some three feet above the deck, through which were led many of the principal ropes used in navigating the ship. The crew squatted around on the deck, or perched on coils of rope and on the gun-carriages, listening attentively, as it was only by so doing that the ballads could be memorized and passed on by word of mouth.

Yea, verily, "Times change and we change with them," despite which Old Ocean will never lack for her wanderers, her adventurers, her artists, her poets, and even her outcasts in the remote corners of the earth, whether they tread the poop-deck, bunk with the "packet-rats" in the fo'c'sle, or join the ranks of the down-and-outs on some coral-ballasted beach in the South Seas. That is what makes a human document of this character so worthy of preservation. As Bill Adams puts it:

"We takes our luck wi' the tough ship, the tall ship,
        the fast ship —
We takes our luck wi' any ship to sign away for sea.
We takes our trick wi' the best o' them,
And sings our song wi' the rest o' them,
When the bell strikes for the dog-watch
An' the moon is on the sea."

R. F.

New York
January, 1924

ACKNOWLEDGMENTS

THE editor acknowledges his indebtedness to the following authors and publishers for the use of copyright poems:

Messrs. Brentano's for "There's Nothing Like a Ship at Sea," "The Remedy," and "The Beachcomber," from *Chanteys and Ballads*, by Harry Kemp.

The Century Company for "The Great Seducer" and "Penang," from *The Sea Poems*, by Cale Young Rice.

The Cornhill Publishing Company for "The World of Ships" and "The Sea Tramp," from *Sea Lanes*, by Burt Franklin Jenness.

Messrs. J. M. Dent and Company, Ltd., London, for "The Port o' Missing Ships" and "The Last Voyage," from *Spun-Yarn and Spindrift*, by Norah M. Holland.

Messrs. Devin, Adair Company for "Freighters," from *Moods and Memories*, by Edmund Leamy.

The Oliver Ditson Company and Mr. Stanton H. King for the musical arrangement of the Sailors' Chanteys.

Messrs. Dodd, Mead and Company for "A Dash to the Pole" and "What Ho! She Blows!" from *Nautical Lays of a Landsman*, by Wallace Irwin; "The Tracks of the Trades," from *In the Tracks of the Trades*, by Lewis R. Freeman; "Sea Song," from *Sea and Bay,* by Charles Wharton Stork; "Drake's Drum," from *Admirals All,* and "Messmates," from *The Island Race,* by Sir Henry Newbolt.

Messrs. George H. Doran Company for "Sea Wind," from *A Banjo at Armageddon,* and "The Destroyer Men," from *Camp and Trench,* by Berton Braley (copyright, 1917–18); "Portrait of a Sailor," and "Sea Mood," from *Spindrift,* by Milton Raison (copyright, 1922); "Ships that Pass," from *Small Craft,* and "The Derelict," from *Rhymes of the Red Ensign,* by C. Fox Smith (copyright, 1919); "Green Escape," from *Chimneysmoke,* by Christopher Morley (copyright, 1917, 1919, 1920, 1923).

Messrs. Doubleday, Page and Company for "The Long Trail," "The Last Chantey," and "Ballad of the Bolivar," from *Collected Poems,* by Rudyard Kipling; "Song for All Seas — All Ships," from *Leaves of Grass,* by Walt Whitman; "With the Submarines," from *Dreams and Dust,* by Don Marquis.

Messrs. E. P. Dutton and Company for "The Port o' Missing Ships" and "The Last Voyage," from *Spun-Yarn and Spindrift,* by Norah M. Holland; "The Tankers," by Gordon Malherbe Hillman, and "The Anchor," by William Laird, from *Contemporary Verse Anthology.*

Messrs. Harper and Brothers for "Out of the Fog," from *Poems,* by Dana Burnet; "The Rush of the Oregon," from *A Ballad-Maker's Pack,* by Arthur Guiterman.

Messrs. William Heinemann, Ltd., London, for

"Alchemy," and "The Reefs," from *The Ballad of the "Royal Ann,"* by Crosbie Garstin.

Messrs. Hodder and Stoughton, Ltd., London, for "The Derelict," from *Rhymes of the Red Ensign,* by C. Fox Smith.

Messrs. Henry Holt and Company for "The Landlubber's Toast," from *Davy Jones' Yarns and Other Salted Songs,* by Thomas R. Ybarra.

Messrs. Robert M. McBride and Company for "West India Dock Road," from *London Lamps,* by Thomas Burke.

The Macmillan Company for "Sea Fever" and "D'Avalo's Prayer," reprinted from *Salt Water Poems and Ballads,* by John Masefield (copyright, 1912, 1913, 1914, by the Macmillan Company; copyright, 1916, by John Masefield); "On First Seeing the Ocean," from *The Quest,* by John G. Neihardt; "The Voyagers," from *Highland Light and Other Poems,* by Henry Adams Bellows.

Mr. Elkin Mathews, London, for "Drake's Drum," from *Admirals All,* and "Messmates," from *The Island Race,* by Sir Henry Newbolt.

Messrs. G. P. Putnam's Sons for "Mariners" and "Shipping News," from *Ships in Harbor,* by David Morton; "Song of the Derelict," from *In Flanders Fields,* by John McCrae.

Messrs. Small, Maynard and Company for "The Sea Gypsy," from *Songs of Vagabondia,* by Richard Hovey.

Messrs. Frederick A. Stokes and Company for "Billy Peg-Leg's Fiddle," "The Stowaway," and "I've Been Dreamin'," from *Fenceless Meadows,* and *Tales of the Sea,* by Bill Adams (copyright,

1923); "Alchemy" and "The Reefs," from *The Ballad of the "Royal Ann,"* by Crosbie Garstin.

Messrs. A. P. Watt and Son, London, and Mr. Kipling for "The Long Trail," "The Last Chantey," and "The Ballad of the Bolivar," from *Collected Poems,* by Rudyard Kipling.

Adventure Magazine for "Service Stripes," by Berton Braley; "A Sailorman's a Free Man," by Archie Austin Coates; "Homeward Bound" and "Below the Line," by William Daniel; "The China Clipper," by Aaron Davis; "Sea Fever," by Mary Carolyn Davies; "The Saving of the 'Cora Andrews,'" by Lewis R. Freeman; "The Wooley," by Richard Butler Glaenzer; "The Lubber," by Carol Hayne; "The Last Harbor," by Helen Ives Gilchrist; "Tramp Steamer Standing Out, Sir," by James V. Murray; "The Incorrigible," by Larry O'Conner; "Abandoned in the Ice," by Chart Pitt; "The Old-Timer," by R. M. Patterson, Jr.; "The Tops'l Schooner," by Kenneth Rand; "The Square Peg," by Gordon Seagrove; "Realization," and "The Seafaring Turn," by Ira South.

The Bookfellows for "The Call of the Seven Seas," from *The Phantom Caravan,* by Kendall Banning.

The Bookman for "The Pirates of Tortuga," by Hermann Hagedorn.

The Century Magazine for "The Old Sailor," by Glenn Ward Dresbach, and "Deep-Water Song," by John Reed.

The Chicago Daily News for "Window Song," by Nancy Shores.

Contemporary Verse for "The Last Ship," by Glenn Ward Dresbach; "Sailing Directions," by Gordon Malherbe Hillman; "The Old Pilot Speaks," by Phœbe Hoffman; "Of Mariners," by Harold Vinal.

Munsey's Magazine for "The Last Port," by John D. Swain.

The Nautical Magazine for "The Derelict's Return," by Lieutenant John Anderson, R.N.R.; "Mercantile Jack," by Harold Begbie.

The New York Evening Post for "Running the Easting Down," by Felix Riesenberg; "Burial at Sea," by A. Binns; "High Tide at 4 A.M." and "Drink to the men who have gone ashore," by William McFee; "'Tusitala's' Christening Ode," by R. D. Turnbull; "A 'Tusitala' Fore-bitter," by W. L. Werner, and "The Leviathan's Three Hundred."

The New York Sun for "Windows over Water," by Leslie Nelson Jennings.

The New York Times for "The Wistful One," by Abigail Cresson; "Euthanasia," by Colby Rucker.

The New York Tribune for "South Sea Stuff," by James J. Montague.

The Outlook for "Haven," by Harold Trowbridge Pulsifer.

Punch, London, for "The Three Ships," by C. Fox Smith; "The Reefs," by Crosbie Garstin.

The Saturday Evening Post for "Ghost Ships," by Gordon Seagrove; "Sailors," by J. Warren Merrill.

Scribner's Magazine for "Taken Ship," by Charles Buxton Going.

The Spectator, London, for " Alchemy," by Crosbie Garstin.

Voices for " Sea-Born," by Harold Vinal.

Mr. Bill Adams for " Johnnie Chantey-Man " and " L'Envoi."

Mr. Thomas Fleming Day for " The Ships " and " The Coasters," from *Songs of Sea and Sail.*

Mr. Charles Buxton Going for " The Master," from *Star-Glow and Song.*

CONTENTS

SONGS OF THE SEA
AND
SAILORS' CHANTEYS

SONGS OF THE SEA
AND SAILORS' CHANTEYS

THE RETURN

I will go back to the great, sweet mother, —
  Mother and lover of men, the Sea.
I will go down to her, I and none other,
  Close with her, kiss her, and mix her with me;
Cling to her, strive with her, hold her fast;
O fair, white mother, in days long past,
Born without sister, born without brother,
  Set free my soul as thy soul is free.

O fair, green-girdled mother of mine,
  Sea, that art clothed with the sun and the rain,
Thy sweet, hard kisses are strong like wine,
  Thy large embraces are keen like pain.
Save me and hide me with all thy waves,
Find me one grave of thy thousand graves,
Those pure, cold, populous graves of thine,
  Wrought without hand in a world without stain.

I shall sleep and move with the moving ships,
  Change as the winds change, veer in the tide;
My lips will feast on the foam of thy lips,
  I shall rise with thy rising, with thee subside;
Sleep, and not know if she be, if she were,
Filled full with life to the eyes and hair,
As a rose is fulfilled to the rose-leaf tips
  With splendid summer and perfume and pride.

This woven raiment of nights and days,
    Were it once cast off and unwound from me,
Naked and glad would I walk in thy ways,
    Alive and aware of thy waves and thee;
Clear of the whole world, hidden at home,
Clothed with the green and crowned with the
        foam,
A pulse of the life of thy straits and bays,
    A vein in the heart of the streams of the Sea.

Fair mother, fed with the lives of men,
    Thou art subtle and cruel of heart, men say;
Thou hast taken and shalt not render again;
    Thou art full of thy dead and cold as they.
But death is the worst that comes of thee;
Thou art fed with our dead, O Mother, O Sea!
But when hast thou fed on our hearts? — or when,
    Having given us love, hast thou taken away?

O tender-hearted, O perfect lover,
    Thy lips are bitter, and sweet thine heart.
The hopes that hurt and the dreams that hover,
    Shall they not vanish away and apart?
But thou, thou art sure, thou art older than earth;
Thou art strong for death and fruitful of birth;
Thy depths conceal and thy gulfs discover;
    From the first thou wert; in the end thou art.
                    Algernon Charles Swinburne

STOWAWAY

I crossed the gangway in the winter's raining,
Late in the night, when it was dreary dark;

The only sounds the rain's hiss, and the com-
   plaining
Of mooring hawsers holding that lean barque.

She sailed before the dawn, the evening found me
A sea-sick nipper hidden in spare sails.
I feared they'd drag me out and maybe drown
   me, —
The barque was trembling, dipping both her rails.

Soon I crept forth. Her long, lee rail was sweeping.
A homing ship drove by with hurrying feet,
A school of porpoises all 'round her leaping,
While stars dipped low, her dizzied spars to greet.

"Three cheers!" they cried, and I could hear their
   voices,
And the sharp beating of her clanged iron bells;
Her music faded, merged in the sea's noises,
And she was gone, loud cheering down the swells.

And in me then a something seemed to waken,
And I was 'mazed. It was as though the sea,
Or the big topsails by the night-wind shaken,
Had cast a sort of magic over me.

The mast-heads reeled. In the bright north the
   Dipper
Hung dazzling diamonds 'round her sails, ghost
   white.
The seas were dim, and the deep-breathing clipper
Quivered her feet, and shook with sheer delight.

    . . . .

It's long ago, my first night on the sea,
And I'm grown old, and sailing days are sped.
And I am waiting, waiting patiently,
Till other topsails gleam above my head.

There'll be a wharf, I know, where I am going,
There'll be a gangway for the likes o' me;
There'll be some lofty packet seaward going, —
They'll be fine ships on that eternal sea!

                      Bill Adams

THE LONG TRAIL

There's a whisper down the field where the year has
       shot her yield,
   And the ricks stand grey to the sun,
Singing: "Over then, come over, for the bee has
       quit the clover,
   And your English summer's done."
      You have heard the beat of the off-shore wind,
      And the thresh of the deep-sea rain;
      You have heard the song — how long? how
       long?
      Pull out on the trail again!
Ha' done with the Tents of Shem, dear lass,
We've seen the seasons through,
And it's time to turn on the old trail, our own
       trail, the out trail,
Pull out, pull out, on the Long Trail — the trail
      that is always new!

It's North you may run to the rime-ringed sun
   Or South to the blind Horn's hate;

Or East all the way into Mississippi Bay,
  Or West to the Golden Gate —
    Where the blindest bluffs hold good, dear lass,
    And the wildest tales are true,
    And the men bulk big on the old trail, our own
      trail, the out trail,
    And life runs large on the Long Trail — the
      trail that is always new.

The days are sick and cold, and the skies are grey
     and old,
  And the twice-breathed airs blow damp;
And I'd sell my tired soul for the bucking beam-sea
     roll
  Of a black Bilbao tramp,
    With her load-line over her hatch, dear lass,
    And a drunken Dago crew,
    And her nose held down on the old trail, our
      own trail, the out trail
    From Cadiz south on the Long Trail — the
      trail that is always new.

There be triple ways to take, of the eagle or the
     snake,
  Or the way of a man with a maid;
But the sweetest way to me is a ship's upon the sea
  In the heel of the North-East Trade.
    Can you hear the crash on her bows, dear lass,
    And the drum of the racing screw,
    As she ships it green on the old trail, our own
      trail, the out trail,
    As she lifts and 'scends on the Long Trail —
      the trail that is always new?

See the shaking funnels roar, with the Peter at the
    fore,
  And the fenders grind and heave,
And the derricks clack and grate, as the tackle
    hooks the crate,
  And the fall-rope whines through the sheave;
    It's "Gang-plank up and in," dear lass,
    It's "Hawsers warp her through!"
    And it's "All clear aft" on the old trail, our
    own trail, the out trail,
    We're backing down on the Long Trail — the
    trail that is always new.

O the mutter overside, when the port-fog holds us
    tied,
  And the sirens hoot their dread,
When foot by foot we creep o'er the hueless, view-
    less deep
  To the sob of the questing lead!
    It's down by the Lower Hope, dear lass,
    With the Gunfleet Sands in view,
    Till the Mouse swings green on the old trail,
    our own trail, the out trail,
    And the Gull Light lifts on the Long Trail —
    the trail that is always new.

O the blazing tropic night, when the wake's a welt
    of light
  That holds the hot sky tame,
And the steady fore-foot snores through the planet-
    powdered floors
  Where the scared whale flukes in flame!

Her plates are flaked by the sun, dear lass,
And her ropes are taut with the dew,
For we're booming down on the old trail, our
own trail, the out trail,
We're sagging south on the Long Trail — the
trail that is always new.

Then home, get her home, where the drunken
rollers comb,
And the shouting seas drive by,
And the engines stamp and ring, and the wet bows
reel and swing,
And the Southern Cross rides high!
Yes, the old lost stars wheel back, dear lass,
That blaze in the velvet blue.
They're all old friends on the old trail, our own
trail, the out trail,
They're God's own guide on the Long Trail —
the trail that is always new.

Fly forward, O my heart, from the Foreland to the
Start —
We're steaming all too slow,
And it's twenty thousand mile to our little lazy isle
Where the trumpet-orchids blow!
You have heard the call of the off-shore wind
And the voice of the deep-sea rain;
You have heard the song — how long — how
long?
Pull out on the trail again!

The Lord knows what we may find, dear lass,
And the Deuce knows what we may do —

But we're back once more on the old trail, our
    own trail, the out trail,
We're down, hull-down, on the Long Trail — the
    trail that is always new!

Rudyard Kipling

SEA-FEVER

I must go down to the seas again, to the lonely sea
    and the sky,
And all I ask is a tall ship and a star to steer her by,
And the wheel's kick and the wind's song and the
    white sail's shaking,
And a grey mist on the sea's face and a grey dawn
    breaking.

I must go down to the seas again, for the call of the
    running tide
Is a wild call and a clear call that may not be denied;
And all I ask is a windy day with the white clouds
    flying,
And the flung spray and the blown spume, and the
    sea-gulls crying.

I must go down to the seas again to the vagrant
    gypsy life,
To the gull's way and the whale's way where the
    wind's like a whetted knife;
And all I ask is a merry yarn from a laughing fellow-
    rover,
And quiet sleep and a sweet dream when the long
    trick's over.

John Masefield

THE SEA WIND

Below the skyline drops the shore,
    The long, grim graybacks lift and fall,
Against the bows they crash and roar,
    The engine throbs, the sea gulls call —
And, salt against my pallid face,
    There comes the challenge bold and free
Of that world-tramp who roams through space,
    The wind — the wind of open sea!

Here is no breeze of drowsy lanes
    Nor breath of crowded towns and stale,
This is the wind that sweeps the mains
    And leaps along the trackless trail,
And with its savor on my lips
    The ancient joy comes back to me,
Of those who dared — in Viking ships —
    The wind — the wind of open sea!

It blows from out the vasty skies
    Across the tumbling sea's expanse,
It stings to deeds of high emprise,
    It sings of glamor and romance;
Chill, clean and strong — my pulses leap,
    My heart is filled with buoyant glee,
I greet the rover of the deep,
    The wind — the wind of open sea!

                                Berton Braley

APOSTROPHE TO THE OCEAN

There is a pleasure in the pathless woods,
There is a rapture on the lonely shore,
There is society where none intrudes
By the deep Sea, and music in its roar:
I love not Man the less, but Nature more,
From these our interviews, in which I steal
From all I may be, or have been before,
To mingle with the Universe, and feel
What I can ne'er express, yet cannot all conceal.

Roll on, thou deep and dark blue Ocean, roll!
Ten thousand fleets sweep over thee in vain;
Man marks the earth with ruin, his control
Stops with the shore; upon the watery plain
The wrecks are all thy deed, nor doth remain
A shadow of man's ravage, save his own,
When, for a moment, like a drop of rain,
He sinks into thy depths with bubbling groan,
Without a grave, unknelled, uncoffined, and un-
        known.

His steps are not upon thy paths, thy fields
Are not a spoil for him, — thou dost arise
And shake him from thee; the vile strength he
        wields
For earth's destruction thou dost all despise,
Spurning him from thy bosom to the skies,
And send'st him, shivering in thy playful spray
And howling, to his Gods, where haply lies
His petty hope in some near port or bay,
And dashest him again to earth:—there let him lay.

The armaments which thunderstrike the walls
Of rock-built cities, bidding nations quake
And monarchs tremble in their capitals,
The oak leviathans, whose huge ribs make
Their clay creator the vain title take
Of lord of thee and arbiter of war, —
These are thy toys and, as the snowy flake,
They melt into thy yeast of waves which mar
Alike the Armada's pride or spoils of Trafalgar.

Thy shores are empires, changed in all save
    thee; —
Assyria, Greece, Rome, Carthage, what are
    they?
Thy waters washed them power while they were
    free,
And many a tyrant since; their shores obey
The stranger, slave or savage; their decay
Has dried up realms to deserts; — not so thou;
Unchangeable save to thy wild waves' play,
Time writes no wrinkle on thine azure brow;
Such as creation's dawn beheld, thou rollest
    now.

Thou glorious mirror, where the Almighty's form
Glasses itself in tempests; in all time,
Calm or convulsed, — in breeze, or gale, or
    storm,
Icing the pole, or in the torrid clime
Dark-heaving; — boundless, endless, and sub-
    lime, —
The image of Eternity, — the throne
Of the Invisible; even from out thy slime

The monsters of the deep are made; each zone
Obeys thee; thou goest forth, dread, fathomless,
    alone.

And I have loved thee, Ocean! and my joy
Of youthful sports was on thy breast to be
Borne like thy bubbles, onward. From a boy
I wantoned with thy breakers, — they to me
Were a delight; and if the freshening sea
Made them a terror, 'twas a pleasing fear;
For I was as it were a child of thee,
And trusted to thy billows far and near,
And laid my hand upon thy mane, — as I do here.
          George Gordon (Lord) Byron

THE CALL OF THE SEVEN SEAS

I hear the call of the wanderlust,
And God knows why, but go I must;
Until my bones are drifting dust
    I'll follow the sea-gull's cry.
The bow-wash song to the dog-watch bell,
The kick o' the wheel and the chantey's spell
Get hold of a man in spite o' Hell,
    And a better man than I!

I've ranged and rogued and I've done my bit;
I've danced the dance and I've paid for it;
I've turned my heel on the Scripture's writ
    In the lure of an alien eye.
But I set no store in the likes o' these;
I want the sweep of the Seven Seas,
The mainsail-haul to a biting breeze
    And a star to steer me by!

And yet — the old dream comes to me
Of a quiet home where I would be
Beyond the trackless miles o' the sea
   And the far-blown clouds o' foam.
My homeland's call sets me astir
With hopes as brave as once they were,
And my heart cries out to the cry of her, —
   For she calls me, this time, home!
               Kendall Banning

" I'VE BEEN DREAMIN' "

I've been dreamin',
Of a randy, dandy clipper with her tops'ls set,
Pitchin' heavy down the westin' with the leeches
    wet.
Billy Newland, the old skipper, from his high bridge
    head,
Shoutin' to us packet rats — an' these the words
    he said:
  "Hop along, now! Loose them 'gallants! Skip
    aloft, now! Jump along!"

Oh, them packet rats were swearin' an' a-breakin'
    into song!
Packet rats a-roarin', "Ranzo," rats a-singin',
    "Roll an' Go,"
Haulin' on them 'gallant braces, cryin', "Blow,
    boys, blow!"

      Let her blow for Frisco city!
        Let the dandy clipper race!
      For them swingin' feet an' pretty
        Of the gals at Tony's place.

Soon we'll see old Tony smilin',
    Hear his gals begin to sing,
Hear old Billy Dick beguilin'
    Music from a fiddle-string!

Oh, there's drowned an' perished clippers
    An' there's rats that died —
But there's gals wi' flowered slippers
    An' their skirts flung wide!

Did you say there ain't no clippers? Did you say
        them days is done?
Days of packet rats an' packets, an' stars an' moon
        an' sun?
O' lights upon the water, a-shinin' on the sea?
My God, but *I'm* a packet rat!
What will become of me?

I've *got* to see tall clippers, I've *got* to sing an' shout
When the 'gallants are mastheaded and the jibs
        are runnin' out.
I've *got* to roar of "Ranzo," an' "Blow, my bullies,
        blow!"
When the ice-cakes heap a-cracklin', an' the Horn
        is lost in snow.
I wants them lights by Frisco, an' lights by Salem
        too,
And dandy skippers swearin' at the signin' of the
        crew.
Red Jacket's gone? And *Dancin' Wave? Guidin'
        Star* as well?
Then what of *Golden Era?* . . . God help me! This
        is hell!

Good-by, farewell, kedge anchor! The shoals lie
   deep about;
The packet rats are singin', an' their chorus dyin'
   out.
The clippers lie a-westin' where the westin' sun
   burns red,
An' the packet rats are restin' in the havens of the
   dead.

Good-by to Dame Romancing an' her dainty
   feathered frock!
Good-by to all the laughter at the swingin' of the
   lock!
Good-by to capstan payments, good-by to ships at
   sea —
If the packets rest a-westin' — ah — westin's right
   for me!

Bill Adams

DERELICT

(*A Reminiscence of "Treasure Island"*)

"The Dead Man's Chest," as is known to exceeding few,
is the name of a treacherous sunken reef in the Caribbean
Sea. The legend upon which Mr. Allison has based his
remarkable poem is to the effect that during that flourish-
ing period of piracy on the " Spanish Main " in the seven-
teenth century a Spanish galleon, returning home heavily
laden with treasure, was raided by a piratical crew who
made every man-jack aboard her walk the plank and
then fell to fighting among themselves over the divi-
sion of the loot. The result of this " free for all " was that
fifteen husky cutthroats set their less powerful compan-
ions adrift in the long-boat with just enough fresh water
and sea-biscuit to last them until they reached the main-
land. The fifteen worthies left in possession of the gal-

leon and its treasure, being no better able to agree among themselves as to its division than their luckless companions whom they had abandoned, started in turn a fight among themselves which resulted in the death of all. The galleon drifted derelict on the Dead Man's Chest, where she was subsequently discovered by those members of the crew who had been set adrift. And — it is the bo's'n's mate who tells the story of the sight which met their eyes as they clambered up the side. — R. F.

Fifteen men on the Dead Man's Chest —
   Yo-ho-ho and a bottle of rum!
Drink and the Devil had done for the rest —
   Yo-ho-ho and a bottle of rum!
The mate was fixed by the bos'n's pike,
The bos'n brained with a marlinspike,
And cookey's throat was marked belike
     It had been gripped
       By fingers ten;
     And there they lay,
       All good dead men,
Like break-o'-day in a boozing-ken —
   Yo-ho-ho and a bottle of rum!

Fifteen men of a whole ship's list —
   Yo-ho-ho and a bottle of rum!
Dead and be-damned and the rest gone whist! —
   Yo-ho-ho and a bottle of rum!
The skipper lay with his nob in gore
Where the scullion's ax his cheek had shore —
And the scullion he was stabbed times four:
     And there they lay,
      And the soggy skies
     Dripped all day long
      In up-staring eyes —

At murk sunset and at foul sunrise —
   Yo-ho-ho and a bottle of rum!

Fifteen men of 'em stiff and stark —
   Yo-ho-ho and a bottle of rum!
Ten of the crew had the murder mark —
   Yo-ho-ho and a bottle of rum!
'Twas a cutlass swipe, or an ounce of lead,
Or a yawing hole in a battered head,
And the scuppers glut with a rotting red:
     And there they lay —
       Aye, damn my eyes!
     All lookouts clapped
       On paradise —
All souls bound just contrariwise —
   Yo-ho-ho and a bottle of rum.

Fifteen men of 'em good and true —
   Yo-ho-ho and a bottle of rum!
Every man-jack could ha' sailed with Old Pew —
   Yo-ho-ho and a bottle of rum!
There was chest on chest full of Spanish gold,
With a ton of plate in the middle hold,
And the cabins riot of loot untold:
     And they lay there
       That had took the plum,
     With sightless glare
       And their lips struck dumb,
While we shared all by the rule of thumb —
   Yo-ho-ho and a bottle of rum!

More was seen through the sternlight screen —
   Yo-ho-ho and a bottle of rum!

Chartings ondoubt where a woman had been —
  Yo-ho-ho and a bottle of rum!
A flimsy shift on a bunker-cot,
With a thin dirk-slot through the bosom spot
And the lace stiff-dry in a purplish blot:
      Or was she wench . . .
        Or some shuddering maid . . .
      That dared the knife
        And that took the blade?
By God! She was stuff for a plucky jade —
  Yo-ho-ho and a bottle of rum!

Fifteen men on the Dead Man's Chest —
  Yo-ho-ho and a bottle of rum!
Drink and the Devil had done for the rest —
  Yo-ho-ho and a bottle of rum!
We wrapped 'em all in a mains'l tight,
With twice-ten turns of a hawser's bight,
And we heaved 'em over and out of sight —
      With a Yo-heave-ho!
        And a fare-you-well!
      And a sullen plunge
        In the sullen swell —
Ten fathoms deep on the road to Hell —
  Yo-ho-ho and a bottle of rum!

                              Young Ewing Allison

"SHIPS THAT PASS"

(An Episode of the Cruiser Patrol)

There are ships that pass in the night-time, some
    poet has told us how,
But a ship that passed in the day-time is the one
    I'm thinking of now,

Where the seas roll green from the Arctic and the
    wind comes keen from the Pole,
'Tween Rockall Bank and the Shetlands, up North
    on the long patrol

We sighted her one day early; the forenoon watch
    was begun,
There was mist like wool on the water, and a
    glimpse of a pale, cold sun,
And she came through the dim, grey weather, — a
    thing of wonder and gleam,
From the port o' the Past on a bowline, close-
    hauled on a wind of dream.

The rust of years was upon her — she was weath-
    ered by many a gale —
The flag of a Dago republic went up to her peak at
    our hail;
But I knew her — Lord God! I knew her, as how
    could I help but know
The ship that I served my time in, no matter how
    long ago!

I'd have climbed to her royals blindfold, I'd have
    known her spars in a crowd;
Aloft and alow, I knew her, brace and halliard and
    shroud —
From the scroll-work under her stern-ports to the
    paint on her figure-head —
And the shout, "All hands!" on her maindeck
    would have tumbled me up from the dead.

She moved like a queen on the water, with the
    grace that was her's of yore,
The sun on her shining canvas — what had she to
    do with war,
With a world that is full of trouble and seas that
    are stained with crime?
She came like a dream remembered, dreamt once
    in a happier time.

She was youth, and its sorrow that passes — the
    light, the laughter, the joy,
The South, and the small white cities, and the care-
    free heart of a boy,
The farewell flash of the Fastnet to light you the
    whole world round,
And the hoot of the tug at parting — and the song
    of the homeward bound, —

The sun, and the flying-fish weather — night, and
    a fiddle's tune,
And palms, and the warm maize-yellow of a low,
    West Indian moon —
Storm in the high South latitudes — and the boom
    of a Trade-filled sail —
And the anchor-watch in the tropics, and the old
    Sou' Spainer's tale.

Was it the lap of the wave I heard or the chill
    wind's cry,
Or a snatch of a deep-sea chanty I knew in the
    years gone by?

Was it the whine of the gear in the sheaves, or the
    seagulls' call,
Or the ghost of my shipmates' voices, tallying on to
    the fall?

.   .   .   .

I went through her papers duly — and no one, I
    hope, could see
A freight of the years departed was the cargo she
    bore for me!
I talked with her Dago captain while we searched
    her for contraband,
And ... I longed for one grip of her wheel-spokes
    like a grip of a friend's right hand.

And I watched while her helm went over, and the
    sails were sheeted home,
And under her moving forefoot the bubbles broke
    into foam,
Till she faded from sight in the greyness — a thing
    of wonder and gleam,
For the port of the Past on a bowline — closehauled
    on a wind of dream!

                    C. Fox Smith

THERE'S NOTHING LIKE A SHIP AT SEA

There's nothing like a ship at sea with all her sails
    full-spread
And the ocean thundering backward 'neath her
    mounting figurehead, —
And the bowsprit plunging starward and then nos-
    ing deep again.
"There's nothing like a ship at sea," Sing Ho! ye
    sailormen.

Oh, a little wayside tavern is a jolly thing to know
Where there's mugs and waiting tables and an
  open fire a-glow;
And it's good to have a song to sing at work as well
  as play;
And it's pleasant to have memories of boyhood's
  yesterday;
And they say a tried companion walking down an
  endless road
Makes the heavy footfall lighter, shares the burden
  of the load . . .
And I see my sweetheart walking with her head
  held proud and high
And I wish that I was with her where the bells ring
  in the sky . . .

But there's nothing like a ship at sea with all her
  sails full-spread
And the ocean thundering backward 'neath her
  mounting figurehead.
Oh, it's once you be a sailor you must go to sea
  again.
"There's nothing like a ship at sea," Sing Ho! ye
  sailormen.

                                          Harry Kemp

WHERE LIES THE LAND?

Where lies the land to which the ship would go?
Far, far ahead, is all her seamen know.
And where the land she travels from? Away,
Far, far behind, is all that they can say.

On sunny noons upon the deck's smooth face,
Linked arm in arm, how pleasant here to pace;
Or, o'er the stern reclining, watch below
The foaming wake far widening as we go.

On stormy nights when wild north-westers rave,
How proud a thing to fight with wind and wave!
The dripping sailor on the reeling mast
Exults to bear, and scorns to wish it past.

Where lies the land to which the ship would go?
Far, far ahead, is all her seamen know.
And where the land she travels from? Away,
Far, far behind, is all that they can say.

Arthur Hugh Clough

SAILING DIRECTIONS

Drive her, drive her westward till she sweeps across
      the line,
Though her shrouds are taut and tattered and her
      decks are deep in brine,
Though the sky is scudding orange and the sea is
      frothing wine —,
          Bring her home!

Give her sail and drive her though the cargo roll
      and shift,
Though the seas come over the counter and the
      wind from the polar drift,
Though the wheel kick and the jibs snap as the
      rollers fall and lift —,
          Bring her home!

Swing her always westward though you cut her rig
      to lace,
Though the green sea rakes her as the steep swells
      race,
Though the salt freeze on the rigging, the fulmar on
      your face —,
                    Bring her home!
                         Gordon Malherbe Hillman

GHOST SHIPS

On still blue nights of darkness and high stars,
    Soft comes a sound as gentle as June rain:
The song of roving winds through bending spars,
    The laugh of risen ships bound out again.
With creamy tops'ls whispering to clean skies,
    And sweet hulls treading old blue water down —
Hulls that have lain where winding seaweed lies
    Deep down, deep down, by many an ancient
      town.

Ah! they return, those foundered gypsy ships.
    Hearing the drum of screws they cannot rest;
Old ports call out and quiet quays and slips,
    There are fair isles to sight, new seas to crest;
And when a night comes stiller than the dawn
    They rise again — and sail forever on.
                         Gordon Seagrove

BELOW THE LINE

Below the Line a rusty tramp is steaming
    Toward Rio and the southern ports I know,

Below the Line the phosphorus is gleaming
   Upon the waves that from her counter flow.
The moon lies low upon the far horizon,
   The torn cloud-drift floats past in streamers fine;
The southern ocean calls, and I am going,
   Somewhere — somewhere below the Line.

Below the Line the tall, slim palms are waving
   As gentle trade-winds blow in from the sea.
Below the Line the murm'ring waves are laving
   Upon a firm white beach so dear to me.
The gulls wheel o'er the smiling, sparkling water,
   And white-clad forms upon the sand recline.
My tropic islands call and I am going
   Somewhere — somewhere below the Line.

Below the Line, mid wild, rank vegetation,
   Huge, hanging creatures shutting out the skies,
Below the Line in mystic meditation
   A graven god looks with stark, staring eyes
Upon the ancient ruins of his city,
   O'errun with mango-tree and tangled vine.
The god and jungle call and I am going
   Somewhere — somewhere below the Line.

Below the Line are shining white-roofed cities
   With plazas where at dusk the maidens stroll;
The native band strums forth its plaintive ditties,
   While on the beach the combers boom and roll.
A haunting fragrance drifts upon the breezes,
   From where low walls thick, flowering plants
      confine.

The southern cities call and I am going,
Somewhere — somewhere below the Line.
William Daniel

THE PORT O' MISSING SHIPS

She lies across the western main,
  Beyond the sunset's rim;
Her quays are packed with reeling mists —
  A city strange and dim:
And silent o'er her harbour bar
  The ghostly waters brim.

No sound of life is in her streets,
  No creak of rope or spar
Comes ever from the water's edge
  Where the great vessels are;
Yet ship by ship steals through the mists
  Across her harbour bar.

There many a good galleon
  Has made her anchor fast,
And many a tall caravel
  Her journeying ends at last;
But no living eye may look upon
  That harbour dim and vast.

For one went down in tropic seas,
  And one put fearless forth
To find her death in loneliness
  'Mid icebergs of the north;
Thus ship by ship and crew by crew
  The ocean tried their worth.

She lies across the western main
   Beyond the sunset's rim,
Her quays are packed with reeling mists —
   A city strange and dim;
And silent o'er her harbour bar
   The ghostly waters brim.

               Norah M. Holland

THE "WILLIAM P. FRYE"

I saw her first abreast the Boston Light
At anchor; she had just come in, turned head,
And sent her hawsers creaking, clattering down.
I was so near to where the hawse-pipes fed
The cable out from her careening bow,
I moved up on the swell, shut steam and lay
Hove to in my old launch to look at her.
She'd come in light, a-skimming up the Bay
Like a white ghost with topsails bellying full;
And all her noble lines from bow to stern
Made music in the wind; it seemed she rode
The morning air like those thin clouds that turn
Into tall ships when sunrise lifts the clouds
From calm sea-courses.

There, in smoke-smudged coats,
Lay funnelled liners, dirty fishing-craft,
Blunt cargo-luggers, tugs, and ferry-boats.
Oh, it was good in that black-scuttled lot
To see the *Frye* come lording on her way
Like some old queen that we had half forgot
Come to her own. A little up the Bay
The Fort lay green, for it was springtime then;

The wind was fresh, rich with the spicy bloom
Of the New England coast that tardily
Escapes, late April, from an icy tomb.
The State-house glittered on old Beacon Hill,
Gold in the sun ... 'Twas all so fair awhile;
But she was fairest — this great square-rigged ship
That had blown in from some far happy isle
On from the shores of the Hesperides.

They caught her in a South Atlantic road
Becalmed, and found her hold brimmed up with
        wheat;
"Wheat's contraband," they said, and blew her
        hull
To pieces, murdered one of our staunch fleet,
Fast dwindling, of the big, old sailing ships
That carry trade for us on the high sea —
And warped out of each harbor in the States.
It wasn't law, so it seems strange to me —
A big mistake. Her keel's struck bottom now
And her four masts sunk fathoms, fathoms deep
To Davy Jones. The dank seaweed will root
On her oozed decks, and the cross-surges sweep
Through the set sails; but never, never more
Her crew will stand away to brace and trim,
Nor sea-blown petrels meet her thrashing up
To windward on the Gulf Stream's stormy rim;
Never again she'll head a no'theast gale
Or like a spirit loom up, sliding dumb,
And ride in safe beyond the Boston Light,
To make the harbor glad because she's come.

                              Jeanne Robert Foster

ALCHEMY

In Seventy-Nine her keel was laid,
She did ten years in the coastal trade,
But since those days she's been a rover
Tramping the Seven Seas all over,
Tramping them back and fore and sideways,
But mostly on uncharted tideways
That honest traders had no word of
And gun-boat captains never heard of.
She's wandered where the pack-ice reaches
Seal-poaching on the Bering beaches;
Up sluggish, soupy jungle rivers,
Where lurk proas, devils and the shivers,
Swapping condemned, corroded rifles
For pearls, spice, gold dust and such trifles.
Off flowery, fairy isles she's hovered
Trading (her customers all covered
By Maxims ranged along her gunnel)
Rigged false masts and a dummy funnel,
Flown the White Cross of Island missioners
Then haled her coppery parishioners —
Despite their frantic supplications —
To bondage on remote plantations,
With bland and icicle effront'ry
She's flown the flag of every country
And changed her name to match her kidney.
She's been the Wallaroo of Sydney;
The Oscar Ohlsen of Carlskrona;
The Santa Fé of Barcelona;
The Kelpie, Leith; Il Ré, Catania;
The Konig Haakon, Christiania —
To give a typical selection.

With paint she's altered her complexion
And practised manifold disguises
Pursuing shady enterprises
All up and down the world's dim edges.
Whilst noble ships have split on ledges
Or drowned on nights of flame and thunder
And eager clippers sailed clean under —
Still she slinks on, battered and rusty,
Her engines lame, her bottom crusty,
Her deckhouse starred with bullet splashes,
Her fo-cs'le scarred with shrapnel gashes,
Loud with her engines' crazy clamor
Into the splendid sunset glamour;
Leaky and foul, accursed and haunted
She staggers onward, nothing daunted,
The oily flame-gilt waters churning,
Her rusty hide all glowing, burning
With her every stay a gleaming wire
And her every porthole flashing fire;
Sun-blazoned into the west goes she,
A golden ship on a golden sea.

Crosbie Garstin

THE LAST PORT

(Old Marblehead Cemetery)

Here sleep the silent captains by their sea.
The shrill Northeaster warns them not; their eyes
No longer scan the ghostly fogs that rise
In silent, swirling menace on their lee.
The Polar Star they can no longer see;
The ancient, salt-encrusted town that lies
Below their hill, means naught to them, grown wise

In the vast offing of Eternity.
No watch they set; the sparrow builds her
    nest
Unheeded; nothing stirs within their breast
At call of water fowl or drone of bee;
And here are other graves amid the rest,
Each with a headstone for the absent guest
Graved with its terse inscription:

        Lost at Sea.

            John D. Swain

"A SAILORMAN'S A FREE MAN"

Before I was a sailor, my life was spent on land;
I lived in crowded cities, and I wore their scarlet
    brand;
But when I shipped it eastwardly, a change came
    over me.
I found that there was nothing like the wide, blue
    sea.

        Refrain
      So let the waves go rolling,
      And let the winds go blow.
      A sailorman's a free man
      As only sailors know.
      The town is neat and handy
      For girls and gaietee,
      But Life is worth the living
      On the wide, blue sea!

I sailed the old Atlantic a dozen times or so;
I swung Cape Horn and coasted it as far as
    Callao;

I saw Siam and India and crossed the China Sea;
I found the land was nothing for the likes of me.

Refrain

A sailorman's a free man, and none can tell him
    "No!"
He packs his bag and ships it anywhere he wants
    to go;
He wanders up and down the world, from cradle to
    the grave
And finds his last Snug Harbor underneath the
    wave.

Refrain

Archie Austin Coates

THE SEA GYPSY

I am fevered with the sunset,
I am fretful with the bay,
For the wander-thirst is on me
And my soul is in Cathay.

There's a schooner in the offing,
With her topsails shot with fire,
And my heart has gone aboard her
For the Islands of Desire.

I must forth again to-morrow!
With the sunset I must be
Hull down on the trail of rapture
In the wonder of the Sea.

Richard Hovey

WINDOW SONG

There's a ship lying in and I'd like to be aboard her.
They're loading her with iron rails and cargo for the
South.
The water-line is rising with the iron that they're
loading,
Down at the docks just inside the harbor mouth.

They'll be sailing in the morning with the black
smoke flying
Back with the head-wind that meets the city smoke.
Blue water rippling with the long swells behind her,
Marking out the path of the blue-water folk.

There's a ship lying in and I'd like to be aboard
her,
Sailing in the morning with her hold full of rails —
Somewhere, long ago, I stood watching at a window
Men loading cargo and a harbor full of sails.

Nancy Shores

THE LAST CHANTEY

"And there was no more sea."

Thus said The Lord in the Vault above the Cheru-
bim,
Calling to the angels and the souls in their
degree:
"Lo! Earth has passed away
On the smoke of Judgment Day.
That Our Word may be established shall We
gather up the sea?"

Loud sang the souls of the jolly, jolly mariners:
"Plague upon the hurricane that made us furl and
flee!
But the war is done between us,
In the deep the Lord hath seen us —
Our bones we'll leave the barracout', and God
may sink the sea!"

Then said the soul of Judas that betrayed Him:
"Lord, hast Thou forgotten Thy covenant with
me?
How once a year I go
To cool me on the floe,
And Ye take my day of mercy if Ye take away the
sea!"

Then said the soul of the Angel of the Off-shore
Wind:
(He that hits the thunder when the bull-mouthed
breakers flee):
"I have watch and ward to keep
O'er Thy wonders on the deep,
And Ye take mine honour from me if Ye take
away the sea!"

Loud sang the souls of the jolly, jolly mariners:
"Nay, but we were angry, and a hasty folk are
we!
If we worked the ship together
Till she foundered in foul weather,
Are we babes that we should clamour for a
vengeance on the sea?"

Then said the souls of the slaves that men threw
     overboard:
  "Kennelled in the picaroon, a weary band were
    we;
    But Thy arm was strong to save,
    And it touched us on the wave,
  And we drowsed the long tides idle till Thy
    Trumpets tore the sea."

Then cried the soul of the stout Apostle Paul to
     God:
  "Once we frapped a ship, and she laboured
    woundily.
    There were fourteen score of these,
    And they blessed Thee on their knees,
  When they learned Thy Grace and Glory under
    Malta by the sea."

Loud sang the souls of the jolly, jolly mariners,
  Plucking at their harps, and they plucked un-
    handily:
    "Our thumbs are rough and tarred,
    And the tune is something hard —
  May we lift a Deepsea Chantey such as seamen
    use at sea?"

Then said the souls of the gentlemen-adventurers—
  Fettered wrist to bar all for red iniquity:
    "Ho, we revel in our chains
    O'er the sorrow that was Spain's;
  Heave or sink it, leave or drink it, we were
    masters of the sea!"

Up spake the soul of a gray Gothavn 'speck-
    shioner —
  (He that led the flinching in the fleets of fair
    Dundee):
    "Ho, the ringer and right whale,
    And the fish we struck for sale!
  Will Ye whelm them all for wantonness that
    wallow in the sea?"

Loud sang the souls of the jolly, jolly mariners,
  Crying: "Under Heaven, here is neither lead or
    lea!
    Must we sing for evermore
    On the windless, glassy floor?
  Take back your golden fiddles and we'll beat to
    open sea!"

Then stooped the Lord, and He called the good sea
    up to Him,
  And 'establishèd his borders unto all eternity,
    That such as have no pleasure
    For to praise the Lord by measure,
  They may enter into galleons and serve Him on
    the sea.

Sun, wind, and cloud shall fail not from the face of it,
  Stinging, ringing spindrift, nor the fulmar flying
    free;
    And the ships shall go abroad
    To the glory of the Lord
  Who heard the silly sailor-folk and gave them
    back their sea!
                    Rudyard Kipling

THE SEA TRAMP

A black hull is lifted on the lee;
She dips — and a strange tramp has passed;
A stately vagabond of the sea,
With lines unbeautiful, and bare of mast;
A ragamuffin on the road of ships;
A wanderer that's bidden to and fro,
To fetch and carry wares as fortune flips
The coin of trade, and tells her where to go.
Oft met at every cross-road of the sea,
And docked in all the ports of all the world;
A hobo, though the tramp ship be,
She holds respect of every flag unfurled.
Though dark of hull, unkempt, and stern and cold;
The barnacles of ages on her plates;
The dust from many countries in her hold,
And men of every nation for her mates,
Yet she may hail to-day from some far place,
And weather out the fiercest gale at sea,
To bring my lady perfume or fine lace,
Or serve her with the choicest brand of tea.
Her musty holds are redolent with scents
Of produce from her many ports of call;
Her being speaks of far-off continents;
And an air of romance permeates it all.
What tales of daring might she not tell;
What tragedies of life before the mast ;
How far the wanderlust might cast its spell —
Could she but speak the truth of cruises past!
Of duty vigils at the pumps at night;
Of mutiny nipped while yet in bud;
Of gaming crews in brawl by lantern light —

And now and then a murder in cold blood.
To-day she unloads coffee from Brazil;
To-morrow takes on wheat for Liverpool;
Free-lancing 'round the globe at someone's will —
A tried and faithful ocean-going fool.
For twenty, thirty, fifty years, or more,
Though fouled by drift and weed of many seas,
She tips the horn of plenty at our door —
That those who scorn the tramp may live at ease.

Burt Franklin Jenness

THE THREE FISHERS

Three fishers went sailing away to the West,
  Away to the West as the sun went down;
Each thought on the woman who loved him the
      best,
    And the children stood watching them out of the
      town;
For men must work, and women must weep,
And there's little to earn, and many to keep,
  Though the harbor bar be moaning.

Three wives sat up in the lighthouse tower
  And they trimmed the lamps as the sun went
      down;
They looked at the squall, and they looked at the
      shower,
    And the night-rack came rolling up ragged and
      brown.
But men must work, and women must weep,
Though storms be sudden, and waters deep,
  And the harbor bar be moaning.

Three corpses lay out on the shining sands
  In the morning gleam as the tide went down,
And the women are weeping and wringing their
    hands
  For those who will never come home to the town;
For men must work, and women must weep,
And the sooner it's over, the sooner to sleep;
  And good-by to the bar and its moaning.

Charles Kingsley

THE PORT O' HEART'S DESIRE

Down around the quay they lie, the ships that sail to
    sea,
On shore the brown-cheeked sailormen they pass
    the jest with me;
But soon their ships will sail away with winds that
    never tire,
And there's one that will be sailing to the Port o'
    Heart's Desire.

The Port o' Heart's Desire, and it's, oh, that port
    for me!
And that's the ship that I love best of all that sail
    the sea;
Its hold is filled with memories, its prow it points
    away
To the Port o' Heart's Desire, where I roamed a
    boy at play.

Ships that sail for gold there be, and ships that sail
    for fame,
And some were filled with jewels bright when from
    Cathay they came;

But give me still yon white sail in the sunset's
    mystic fire,
That the running tides will carry to the Port o'
    Heart's Desire.

It's you may have the gold and fame, and all the
    jewels, too,
And all the ships, if they were mine, I'd gladly give
    to you;
I'd give them all right gladly, with their gold and
    fame entire,
If you would set me down within the Port o'
    Heart's Desire.

Oh, speed you, white-winged ships of mine, oh,
    speed you to the sea,
Some other day, some other tide, come back again
    for me;
Come back with all the memories, the joys, and
    e'en the pain,
And take me to the golden hills of boyhood once
    again.

John S. McGroarty

THE MASTER

I have lured him with opaline light
And sung him to confident sleep —
And then — in the horror of night,
I have strangled his cry in the deep.

I have purred at his feet on the sand
And whispered, caressing his sail,

Till, far from the sheltering land,
I might drive him to death in the gale.

I have promised him substance and store
If he gave me his sons and his fleet —
And then — having cozened him sore,
I have flung up his dead at his feet.

I have trapped him with fog and with shoal —
Yet, by line and by light and by sound
He drives, undismayed, to his goal —
He makes me his road the world 'round.

He spans me with log and with lead;
He brands me with marks for his ken —
He buries the tale of his dead
And turns his ships seaward again!

Charles Buxton Going

THE WISTFUL ONE

My window opens upon the sea
And the smell of the sea comes in to me —
And the voice of the sea that calls and calls,
And the sea's hands beating upon my walls.

Sometimes I wake in the night and hear
The sound of the sea, and it seems so near
That I wonder how I have strength of will
To listen and listen and lie so still.

I wonder how I can stay in bed
With a smoth'ring ceiling over my head!

I envy the men who can dip and ride
And drown, if they will, in the brown, salt
    tide.

Oh, why is a half-grown lad so free
To pack up his clothes and put out to sea,
While a maid must live out her life on shore
Mending and washing and sweeping the floor?

Some moonless night, when the sky is black,
I'll run away and I'll never come back;
And maybe the girl who used to be me
Will be far away, like a lad, at sea!

Abigail Cresson

'MARINERS

Men who have loved the ships they took to sea,
    Loved the tall masts, the prows that creamed
        with foam,
Have learned, deep in their hearts, how it might be
    That there is yet a dearer thing than home.
The decks they walk, the rigging in the stars,
    The clean boards counted in the watch they
        keep, —
These, and the sunlight on the slippery spars,
    Will haunt them ever, waking and asleep.

Ashore, these men are not as other men;
    They walk as strangers through the crowded
        street,
Or, brooding by their fires, they hear again
    The drone astern, where gurgling waters meet,

Or see again a wide and blue lagoon,
And a lone ship that rides there with the moon.
David Morton

SERVICE STRIPES

When she was new and splendid, all gleaming
    white and gold,
With millionaires upon her decks and baggage in
    her hold,
The fishing captains swore at her, the skippers of
    the tramps
Shook horny fists in passing and damned her glit-
    tering lamps;
"A bloomin' purse-proud autocrat," they called her
    in their wrath,
"That thinks she owns the right of way along the
    ocean path,"
And then — the war-clouds filled the sky, a vast
    and crimson blur,
And workmen took this lady fair and strangely
    altered her.

Her ports were sealed and painted and guns set
    fore and aft,
Her sides were wildly camouflaged with weird and
    cunning craft,
And in her sumptuous smoking-rooms and dining-
    rooms de luxe
Which once had sheltered plutocrats and baronets
    and dukes,
The dusty brown of khaki cloth was all that met the
    gaze —

The garb of grim adventurers who sought the con-
flict's blaze;
From upper deck to lower deck, from stem to
throbbing stern
Were soldiers, soldiers khaki-clad wherever one
might turn.

And now the war is over, she's white and gold
again,
But captains of the dingy tramps and grizzled
fishermen
Salute her as she races by: "The beauty!" so they
say,
"She sure has won her service stripes, so give her
right of way!
A thoroughbred, that lady, and lookut how she runs,
No wonder that she gave the laugh to all the
bloomin' Huns!
The Liner she's a Lady, but a Lady true an' brave
An' we drop our colors to her as she shoots along
the wave!"

Berton Braley

THE DERELICT'S RETURN

Oh, blink, ye lights, from each familiar headland,
We're glad to make our homing in the dark:
Oh, blink, ye bonnie, bonnie lights of England,
Ye wot not of the number of our bark.

We're six years out, O Christ! we have a story;
Our weed-grown sheathing wallows through the
foam,

We're loaded deep with sin and memories gory,
Oh, blink, ye bonnie lights and let us home.

Our rudder's gone, our compass lies like Satan.
We sold our sails to cheat the winds of God,
We ran bare-poles through winds without abatin';
Our backs are raw beneath the iron rod.

We burned our boats to save our bones from
     freezing;
In Hell's own port we pawned our anchor chains.
The very women shamed us with their teasing,
And jeered to see our toiling in the rains.

We dealt in rotten gear and putrid rations;
Our masts and yards have long gone by the board,
We've kept afloat with "soul-an'-body lashin's,"
And trusting to the mercy of the Lord.

Our decks are rotting with the slime of ages,
We kept no reck'ning, and we laid no course;
Our log-book's filled with mildew and blank pages;
We drift beneath the ensign of remorse.

Oh, but we're water-logged and plague-infected,
The rats have left us, yet we do not sink.
If only we could get repairs effected,
There's time to prick a truer chart, we think.

Then blink in hope, ye lights from windy beacons,
The chandlers' stores lie hard beneath our lee.
While we can swim our courage never weakens,
Oh, fit us out — and we will put to sea.
              Lieut. John Anderson, R.N.R.

THE CHEER OF "THE TRENTON"

A Samoan Memory — 1889

An English opinion. — Consider the scene and the matchless heroism and generosity of this Yankee crew. Almost sure of instant death themselves, they could appreciate the Queen's ship fighting the hurricane and the gallantry of the effort, with the generosity of true mariners. We do not know in all naval records any sound which makes a finer music upon the ear than the cheer of the *Trenton's* men. It was distressed manhood greeting triumphant manhood, the doomed saluting the saved. It was pluckier and more human than any cry raised upon the deck of a victorious line-of-battle ship. It never can be forgotten, must never be forgotten, by Englishmen speaking of Americans. That dauntless cheer to the *Calliope* was the expression of immortal courage. — *London Telegraph.*

Our anchors drag and our cables surge
　　At every shock of the hurtling sea,
While the mist of breakers veils the verge
　　Of the reef of coral under our lee.

From east by north to the north — north west
　　The wild typhoon veers sweep on sweep,
And from moment to moment the cross-wave's
　　　　crest
　　Buries our waist in its sidelong leap.

Under the blows of our plunging screw
　　The whitening breakers foam and churn,
But for all that steam and steel can do
　　We are drifting slowly, astern, astern.

On our starboard quarter, close aboard
  We can see the stanch *Calliope* loom,
While the black flood from her smoke-stack
     poured,
  Covers the sea like a pall of doom.

Her topmasts struck and her yards braced sharp,
  She is headed out for the open main,
While the shrouds like the strings of a giant harp,
  Scream to the touch of the hurricane.

We, from our flag-ship *Trenton's* decks,
  Are watching her battle in hope and dread,
As she threads the throng of the tossing wrecks,
  Now beaten backward, now forging ahead.

She with the red-cross ensign aloft,
  And we, our starry banner below,
Lie beam to beam, as the frigates oft
  Ranged in old sea-fights long ago.

We watch the weight of the tempest fall
  On her flooded decks and her reeling bow,
And our hearts are beating one and all,
  For we both go down should she foul us now.

Through the darkest night there's a gleam to break;
  Fathom by fathom she forges past,
Till we know by the swirl of her eddying wake,
  That her seaward struggle is won at last.

The Admiral tosses his seacap high,
  And from station to station is passed the word,

And over the uproar of wave and sky
   The thunder roll of our cheer is heard.

And back from the Briton's taffrail came
   The gallant, grateful and proud reply,
That stirred our hearts like a pulse of flame —
   The seaman's and brother's last good-bye.

Oh, blood is thicker than water, and long
   Will England's memory hold it dear,
And the tale be told in fo'-c'sle song
   Of the flagship *Trenton's* parting cheer.
                Walter Mitchell

A SONG OF THE FREEBOOTERS

"And how did the Dead Man live his life,
       Mistress Sea?"
"The Dead Man's life with blood was red, as the
     curtains o'er Death's bridal bed,
And the hands of the Slain have cursed his head
       From out of me."

Then here's to the Bight where the Sea-wolves be,
Here's to the Salt Sea's liturgy:
   Yo! for the song that the Dead Man sang,
   Ho! for the gibbet that feels him hang!
And he bows to the moon while the shadows flee;
Here's to the Salt Sea's liturgy!

Some for the Pennon of the *Good Queen Bess*,
Ours is a service — masterless.
   Tho' Death is the Port on the Devil's cruise,
   And the timbers strain in the Good Ship's thews,

Life is as free as a hawk from the jess,
Ours is a service — masterless.

One is gone — but the rest are ten,
Up with the glasses, Gentlemen!
   Up! with a rouse to the Dead Man — he
   Still with the Band keeps company.
To one more brawl on the Sea, and then —
But, up with the glasses, Gentlemen!

"And what shall light the Dead Man's Feast,
                Mistress Sea?"
"The Table's spread when Death is done, this
        is the light that shines thereon:
The Eyes outplucked from the Slaughtered One
            For such as he!"
                    Eugene R. White

SONG OF THE DERELICT

Ye have sung me your songs, ye have chanted your
        rimes
   (I scorn your beguiling, O sea!)
Ye fondle me now, but to strike me betimes.
   (A treacherous lover, the sea!)
Once I saw as I lay, half-awash in the night
A hull in the gloom — a quick hail — and a light
And I lurched o'er to leeward and saved her for
        spite
   From the doom that ye meted to me.

I was sister to *Terrible,* seventy-four,
   (Yo ho! for the swing of the sea!)

And ye sank her in fathoms a thousand or more
  (Alas! for the might of the sea!)
Ye taunt me and sing me her fate for a sign!
What harm can ye wreak more on me or on mine?
Ho, braggart! I care not for boasting of thine —
  A fig for the wrath of the sea!

Some night to the lee of the land I shall steal,
  (Heigh-ho, to be home from the sea!)
No pilot but Death at the rudderless wheel,
  (None knoweth the harbor as he!)
To lie where the slow tide creeps hither and fro
And the shifting sand laps me around, for I know
That my gallant old crew are in Port long ago —
  For ever at peace with the sea!

John McCrae

WE'LL GO TO SEA NO MORE

O, blithely shines the bonny sun
  Upon the Isle of May,
And blithely comes the morning tide
  Into St. Andrew's Bay.
Then, up, gudeman, the breeze is fair
  And up, my braw bairns three;
There's gowd in yonder bonny boat
  That sails sae weel the sea!
    When haddocks leave the Firth o' Forth
      An' mussels leave the shore,
    When oysters climb up Berwick Law,
      We'll go to sea no more —
        No more,
      We'll go to sea no more.

I've seen the waves as blue as air,
  I've seen them green as grass;
But I never feared their heaving yet,
  From Grangemouth to the Bass.
I've seen the sea as black as pitch,
  I've seen it white as snow;
But I never feared its foaming yet,
  Though the winds blew high or low.
    When squalls capsize our wooden walls,
      When the French ride at the Nore,
    When Leith meets Aberdour half-way,
      We'll go to sea no more —
          No more,
      We'll go to sea no more.

I never liked the landsman's life,
  The earth is aye the same;
Gie me the ocean for my dower,
  My vessel for my hame.
Gie me the fields that no man plows,
  The farm that pays no fee;
Gie me the bonny fish that glance
  Sae gladly through the sea.
    When sails hang flapping on the masts
      While through the waves we snore,
    When in a calm we're tempest-tossed,
      We'll go to sea no more —
          No more,
      We'll go to sea no more.

The sun is up and 'round Inchkeith
  The breezes saftly blaw;

The gudeman has the lines on board, —
   Awa, my bairns, awa!
An' ye be back by gloamin' gray,
   An' bright the fire will low,
An' in your tales and sangs we'll tell
   How weel the boat ye row.
     When life's last sun gaes feebly doon
     An' death comes to oor door,
    When a' the world's a dream to us,
     We'll go to sea no more, —
       No more,
     We'll go to sea no more.

Miss Corbett

MESSMATES

He gave us all a good-bye cheerily
   At the first dawn of day;
We dropped him down the side full drearily
   When the light died away.
It's a dead, dark watch that he's a-keeping there,
And a long, long night that lags a-creeping there,
Where the Trades and the tides roll over him
   And the great ships go by.

He's there alone with green seas rocking him
   For a thousand miles around;
He's there alone with dumb things mocking him,
   And we're homeward bound.
It's a long, lone watch that he's a-keeping there,
And a dead, cold night that lags a-creeping there,
While the months and the years roll over him
   And the great ships go by.

I wonder if the tramps come near enough,
  As they thrash to and fro,
And the battleships' bells ring clear enough
  To be heard down below;
If through all the lone watch that he's a-keeping
      there,
And the long, cold night that lags a-creeping there,
The voices of the sailor-men shall comfort him
  When the great ships go by?

Sir Henry Newbolt

A SEA DIRGE

Full fathom five thy father lies:
  Of his bones are coral made;
Those are pearls that were his eyes:
  Nothing of him that doth fade
But doth suffer a sea-change
Into something rich and strange.
Sea-nymphs hourly ring his knell:
Hark! now I hear them, —
        Ding, dong, bell.

Shakespeare

THE REMEDY

When you've failed with ordered people, when
      you've sunk neck-deep again
In the sluggish wash and jetsam of the slackened
      tides of men,
Don't get old and mean and bitter, — there's a
      primal remedy —
Just take a ship to sea, my lad, just take a ship to sea.

There are shipmen grey and agèd but still full of
    ancient mirth,
And they drew their joy of living, not from rooting
    in the earth,
But from striking out forever with a sail that's
    never furled,
And by seeing all the oceans and the wonder of the
    world;
In the dim, Phœnician days and in the wild sea-
    times of old
Do you think they only voyaged for the red of shin-
    ing gold?
No, they slid beyond the sky-line for they felt it
    good to be
On a ship that tramped with thunder down the
    highways of the sea.

When you've drunk the lees of failure, when
    you've fought and never won,
When you've cursed the stale recurrence of the
    certain, weary sun
And the daily, fruitless struggle pledging youth for
    usury,
Come, and cast the world behind you, and take ship
    for open sea;

All you'll need will be your dunnage and your knife
    upon your hip,
And you'll find a bunk that waits you in the fo'c'sle
    of a ship,
And you'll find the wind about you and the ever-
    lasting sky

Leaning huge from four horizons as the flying scud
    blows by —
And you'll find the ancient healing, ever waiting,
    ever free,
That all men have found forever in the sailing of
    the sea.

Harry Kemp

THE SEAFARING TURN

I swore when I had done my hitch,
  That I was through with toil;
Four years' grind was one man's share
  Of "black-gang" grime and oil.
So I "doped" it out to stop ashore
  In a little port we'd made
One lazy cruise in southern seas,
  A harbor where we laid.

For I recalled the fragrant groves,
  The sound of wind-stirred cane,
And the soft blue mist, seen out at sea,
  Of rambling showers of rain.

But no more'n I'd got a bullock cart,
  And roofed my hut with thatch,
And set me down with my old pipe
  Beside my plantain patch,
To idle out my days, when then
  I missed the big ship's bell,
My kit of tools, my oiling can
  And the work I knew so well.

Nor I had not forgot my vow,
And how I used to curse,
The rusty tramp I sailed upon,
— The old sea-going hearse!

But hard tasks challenge able hands
With dares that can't be shirked,
And machinery's like a woman's ways,
A puzzle to be worked.
And — won by stern apprenticeship, —
The man who knows his trade
Will always love his cunning tools,
His own skill he has made.

So while a battered ship limps out
— Which is long as owners be,
With a junk-pile engine in her hull,
I cannot quit the sea.

Ira South

THE GREAT SEDUCER

Who looks too long from his window
At the gray, wide, cold sea,
Where breakers scour the beaches
With fingers of sharp foam;
Who looks too long thro the gray pane
At the mad, wild, bold sea,
Shall sell his hearth to a stranger
And turn his back on home.

Who looks too long from his window —
Tho his wife waits by the fireside —

At a ship's wings in the offing,
At a gull's wings on air,
Shall latch his gate behind him,
Though his cattle call from the byre-side,
And kiss his wife — and leave her —
And wander everywhere.

Who looks too long in the twilight,
Or the dawn-light, or the noon-light,
Who sees an anchor lifted
And hungers past content,
Shall pack his chest for the world's end,
For alien sun — or moonlight,
And follow the wind, sateless,
To Disillusionment!

Cale Young Rice

JOHNNIE CHANTEY-MAN

Johnnie Parrot, Johnnie Parrot, I'll not hear again
That old voice of yours a-ringin' down the windy
    rain,
When the ocean morning's clearin' an' the gale is
    past,
An' we're all a-"yo-heave-ho-in'" by the big
    main mast.

Johnnie Parrot, Johnnie Parrot, I can see 'em
    now —
Southeast trade wind seas a-breakin' high about
    the bow.
I can see the yellow oilskins of a shoutin' crew,
And the "Roll the cotton, bullies, roll her," led by
    you.

I can see the skipper leanin' on the bridge's rail;
Hear him holler to the chief mate, "Crowd her —
 set all sail!"
I can feel the clipper leapin', as a colt untried,
Free to roam the rollin' pastures o' the open tide.

I see the China steward, the nigger cookie's face;
There's a skysail ship to loo'ard, an' we're goin' to
 race;
But a black squall comes a-hidin' all the sea an' sky,
An' white horses run a-ridin' with their manes
 blown high.

I can feel the packet tremble as she lifts her feet,
An' her dainty bows go dancin' down the sea's wide
 street;
I hear Johnnie Parrot singin', singin', "Roll an'
 go!"
An' the sons o' forty seaports roarin', "Yo-
 heave-ho!"

There are girls in forty seaports, an' they wait for
 you —
Wait for Johnnie Chantey-man an' all his singin'
 crew;
But they'd better deck their tresses with bright
 ribbons gay,
An' forget those sailors singin' down the sea's cold
 way.

For the hungry seas are breakin' with an angry roar,
An' there's black squalls blowin' pipin' past a coral
 shore.

There's a clipper lyin' broken like a lily fair —
Lady, take some other token for your lovely hair!

'Tain't no use to love a sailor nor to wait the
　　day
For your Johnnie's chanteys cheery ringin' down
　　the bay!　.
'Tain't no use to listen, lady, for your seaman's
　　love —
Johnnie's drownded, lyin' drownded, in a mer-
　　maid's cove.

Bill Adams

MERCANTILE JACK

An old Red Duster flying from an old "eight-
　　hundred" tramp,
Just like a rag a woman takes to wipe an oily lamp;
A tag of has-been bunting, a soot-stained splash of
　　pride,
But somehow full of glory as it streamed above the
　　tide.
An old Red Duster tugging at its halyards in the
　　stern,
Above the boiling lather of the screw's incessant
　　turn,
With God's white stars above it, which blinked as
　　tho' afraid,
Hummed friendly to a grimy hand a song of British
　　trade: —

　　Up and down the ocean,
　　　All the world for sale,

Shifting tons of merchandise,
   Riding out the gale,
Doing what our fathers did —
   Everything but fail.

Sometimes there's a racket,
   Sometimes there's a spill,
But nothing ever stopped us yet
   And nothing ever will.

The vastness of the ocean, and the wonder of the
      sky,
No meaning had for Grimy as the waves went
      flopping by.
The tramp steamed onward, outward, but his
      thoughts they didn't roam
From his wife and brood of youngsters tucked up
      comfy in his home;
Then the old Red Duster clattered through the
      darkness and the breeze: —
"Your wife won't do no shopping if I'm wiped from
      off the seas!"
And Grimy felt a baby hand creep warmly in his
      own,
And — "Fritz be blowed!," he bellowed out,
      "We'll cross the Danger Zone!"

"Carry on's" the order,
   "Carry on's" the job,
Full of stuff from anywhere,
   Fetched for Britain's mob.
Mother cutting bread and scraps,
   Kettle on the hob.

Gather round the table,
  How's my dear old pal?
Nothing ever stopped us yet
  And nothing ever shall.

Now, say a prayer, Britannia, for him who's on the sea
To fetch you wool and cotton, to bring you corn and
      tea;
There's not a shop you enter in, but oughtn't now
      to mean
A shrine at which to thank Lord God for your
      Mercantile Marine.
They're losing lots of tonnage, and they're losing
      more than kits,
But night and day they're on the sea in spite of
      Pirate Fritz,
The best man holds the ocean, the best man, white
      or black,
Is the man who flies the Duster — God go with you,
      lawful Jack.

        "Carry on," the glory,
          "Carry on," the fame,
        Wiser than your fathers,
          Better at the game;
        Britain in your keeping —
          Guard her sacred name.

        All her life and honour
          Stowed with you aboard!
        Only God can stop you,
          Only God reward.
                              Harold Begbie

WEST INDIA DOCK ROAD

Black man, white man, brown man, yellow man,
  All the lousy Orient loafing on the quay;
Hindoo, Dago, Jap, Malay and Chinaman
  Dipping into London from the great green sea!

Black man, white man, brown man, yellow man,
  Pennyfields and Poplar and Chinatown for me!
Stately moving cutthroats and many colored
    mysteries;
  Never were such lusty things for London days to
    see!

On the evil twilight, rose and star and silver,
  Steals a song that long ago in Singapore they
    sang;
Fragrant of spices, of incense and opium,
  Cinnamon and aconite, the betel and the bhang.

Three miles straight lies lily-clad Belgravia,
  Thin-lipped ladies and padded men and pale.
But here are turbaned princes and velvet-glancing
    gentlemen,
  Tomtom and shark knife and salt-caked sail.

Then get you down to Limehouse, by rigging,
    wharf and smokestack,
  Glamour, dirt and perfume, and dusky men and
    gold;
For down in lurking Limehouse there's the blue
    moon of the Orient,
  Lamps for young Aladdins and bowies for the bold.
                                    Thomas Burke

THE CHINA CLIPPER

A ghost ship drives on the haunted trails:
   Sing Johnny-O and let her go!
She's a lady ship by the way she sails:
   Sing Johnny off to China.

The trade wind strums on the weather shrouds,
   The white seas race astern;
She'll make Foochow like a drift of clouds
   When Winter's on the turn.

By the London docks from Java Head,
   Full half the world away,
She'll back her yards when the dawn is red,
   Two hundred miles a day.

The scent of heathen merchandise,
   The breath of the new Spring tea,
Ivory and silk and jade and rice
   Are a perfumed memory.

A dream ship drives through the misty seas:
   Sing Johnny don't forget her!
She's a lady, sir, and, if you please,
   Sing Johnny off to China.
   Sing Johnny-O and let her go!
   Sing Johnny back from China!

Aaron Davis

THE DESTROYER MEN

There's a roll and pitch and a heave and hitch
   To the nautical gait they take,

For they're used to the cant of the decks aslant
   As the white-toothed combers break
On the plates that thrum like a beaten drum
   To the thrill of the turbines' might,
As the knife-bow leaps through the yeasty deeps
   With the speed of a shell in flight!

Oh! their scorn is quick for the crews who stick
   To a battleship's steady floor,
For they love the lurch of their own frail perch
   At thirty-five knots or more.
They don't get much of the drills and such
   That the battleship jackies do,
But sail the seas in their dungarees,
   A grimy destroyer's crew.

They needn't climb at their sleeping time
   To a hammock that sways and bumps,
They leap — kerplunk! — in a cosy bunk
   That quivers and bucks and jumps.
They hear the sound of the seas that pound
   On the half-inch plates of steel
And close their eyes to the lullabies
   Of the creaking frame and keel.

They scour the deep for the "subs" that creep
   On their dirty assassin's work,
And their keenest fun is to hunt the Hun
   Wherever his U-boats lurk.
They live in hope that a periscope
   Will show in the deep sea swell,
Then a true shot hits and it's "Good-bye, Fritz" —
   His future address is Hell!

They're a lusty crowd and they're vastly proud
     Of the slim, swift craft they drive,
Of the roaring flues and the humming screws
     Which make her a thing alive.
They love the lunge of her surging plunge
     And the murk of her smoke-screen, too,
As they sail the seas in their dungarees,
     A grimy destroyer's crew!

Berton Braley

TO AN OLD BARGE

Soggy in an oily slip, beyond the river's bend
She lay in grimy loneliness and waited for the
     end;
With all her silver canvas that strange suns looked
     upon
Disposed to river Shylocks, and her proud masts
     gone.

Only their ragged stumps remained, and gloomy
     and begrimed
Looked up into the windy skies where royal sonce
     had climbed;
And bows, once so immaculate, were daubed with
     river brown —
The slender, snowy, roving bows that tramped blue
     water down!

Cast out by those who loved her and knew her very
     soul
To traverse dirty rivers and ferry dirty coal —

She lay there by the string-piece, bedraggled,
    without name,
And seemed a wasted beauty forgotten in her
    shame.

And all the men that came and went spit brown
    upon her rails
Where proud-lipped skippers once had leaned and
    eyed the straining sails.
They wheeled their barrows on her decks to please
    a hairy boss —
The decks that gleamed to northern lights and
    sought the Southern Cross.

But one, still strange to landsman's work, rubbing
    a sooty eye,
Gulped: "Cripes — it is the Albemarle — my
    ship — come 'ere to die!"
And dropped his barrow on the plank, stalling the
    men below,
His hat off, his head bowed, for the beauty of long
    ago.

Gordon Seagrove

THE OLD-TIMER

Here I am, an old 'un, a-sittin' on a string-piece,
A-smokin' and a-thinkin' of the days gone by;
Watchin' the steamers a-comin' in or goin' out,
Foulin' the river, and a-blurrin' of the sky —
Lord! What a change has come about, thinks I,

Since I was a young chap — as trim a proper sailor-
man
As ever rove a block or laid a hand upon a clew —
Comin' in from Callao up this very river,
But cleaner then, and clearer, and the sky more
blue,
In the old *Althea* clipper, battered, weary, overdue.

Mary, when I come ashore, told how she watched
her standin' in,
Roundin' to at anchorage — her spars ag'in' the
west,
"Like a fowl from a long flight come back home
ag'in — "
Says Mary — "folds her wings and snuggles down
upon her nest — "
Drop our hook and furl our canvas — "fold our
wings and go to rest."

Mary, she's gone; and the old *Althea*
Is doin' shameful duty as a sand-barge tow.
And me, the proper sailorman, well, I'm wharf
watchman,
A-sittin' here and starin' at the water's ebb and
flow —
A-dreamin' of that Summer evening forty years ago.
                                    R. M. Patterson, Jr.

SAILORS

" They that go down to the sea in ships." — Psalms cvii, 23

Down to the sea in their crazy ships
Went the sailors David knew,

Swarthy and bearded, lean and browned,
　A rough-necked, hard-boiled crew.
They had no compass, they took no sun,
　They steered by a star — or a guess.
They sailed when they could and rowed when they
　　　must
　(Which was rather more than less);
And they cursed the skipper and cursed the grub,
　And on every voyage they swore
That if ever again they got to port
　They would sail the sea no more.

But the very next voyage the same old crew
　Would be found on the same old tub,
Taking again the same old chance
　And cursing the same old grub.
Out from Tyre with precious silks
　They ventured a chartless sea,
And somehow or other they made at last
　The haven where they would be.
And back to Tyre with gold they came,
　And ivory, spice and myrrh,
And swore their vessel might sink or rot
　For they'd sail no more in her.

Now David is dead and his bones are dust
　And his glories passed away,
But they that went down to the sea in his ships
　Are in strange new ships today.
Mighty marvels of steel and steam,
　They race the foiled seas through,
And they tame the lightning to lend them aid —
　But the crew is the same old crew;

And they curse the skipper and curse the grub,
  And in language strong and plain
They swear they will never — the voyage once
      done —
  Go down to the sea again.

The skies of the future may fill with fleets
  That dart while the slow ships creep,
But David's sailors will stick to the sea,
  Where freights though slow will be cheap.
And ever more to the end of time,
  As long as a keel shall swim,
A man shall go down to the sea in a ship.
  (May the Lord be good to him!)
He shall curse his skipper and curse his grub,
  And swear as he always swore;
He will be — unblessed — if he sails again
  When once he is safe ashore.

                              J. Warren Merrill

HAVEN

Give me to rest in a quiet town
Built by old rovers of the sea,
Where they have come to lay them down
Sure of their spirits' mastery.

On shaded streets along the sands
Are white-walled homes where strong men dwell,
And the presence of far-off lands
Born of the sounding harbor bell.

There is the peace of tasks well done,
Of faith true kept with high emprise.

This I ask when my race be run, —
To share the light in seamen's eyes!
Harold Trowbridge Pulsifer

THE OLD SAILOR

A white cloud drifts to meet a sail at sea
  Come in from ports that one may yearn to know,
And here beside the road a slanted tree
  Seems peering down on splendors tossed below.
Beneath the shade a deeper shadow stirs,
  A vagabond gives voice unto his dream,
He says, "My ship had wider sails than hers;
  But see, still distant, how they strain and gleam."
Now in his rags as tattered as the sails,
  Blown in on rocks of some disastrous shore,
He walks a road beside the sea and hails
The ships that left him strong of arm no more.
  At farms, a little inland, where he begs,
  He blusters still and walks with seaman's legs.
Glenn Ward Dresbach

A "TUSITALA" FORE-BITTER *

Come all you gallant seamen now and listen to my
    song:
It's well worth your attention and I will not keep
    you long:

* The full-rigged ship "Tusitala" has had a checkered career. She was launched as the "Inveruglas," at Greenock, Scotland, in 1883. Subsequently she came under Norwegian ownership and was re-named "Sophie." After lying idle in Hampton Roads for over two years, she was bought, in April, 1923, by the Three Hours for Lunch Club, Inc., an organization of New York writers, artists, sculptors, and business men who had her reconditioned, put under American

The wind was booming nor'nor'east in nineteen
    twenty-three,
When on New York horizon rose a clipper from the
    sea.

Some Scotchmen and some pirates came a-tramp-
    ing from her deck;
They rolled along the sidewalks in the wake of Alan
    Breck.

The tenements frowned down on them, but fast
    they marched along;
They stumbled through the canyons and they sang
    a hellish song.

They sang a song that echoed loud along the tallish
    walls,
And sounded through the city like a thousand
    trumpet calls.

A million white-cheeked fellows left their swivel
    chairs and stools;
A million denimed workmen threw aside their ugly
    tools.

A million girls a-sighing left the shop and factoree:
A million boys ran out of school and tossed their
    caps in glee.

registry, and rechristened "Tusitala" in memory of Robert Louis
Stevenson whose effigy she bears as a figure-head. She is now
being operated as a cargo carrier and will eventually be fitted out
with limited passenger accommodations for club members and
their friends.

Oh, the ladies left their scrubbing and policemen
    left their beats
To march behind the pirates down the dirty narrow
    streets.

They went along the narrow streets until they
    reached the ship,
And saw a man with a wooden leg, with pistols on
    his hip.

They trembled and they shivered and they stum-
    bled and they shrank,
For his single eye was on 'em as they crowded up
    the plank.

They crowded up and filled the deck, the cabin, and
    the hold —
Their families were waiting with the supper getting
    cold.

The ship hove up her anchor, not a soul was left
    behind —
Their children cried at home for them, their lonely
    ladi s pined.

The ship set out across the sea, it left the beaten
    track,
And no one ever saw it and it never came back.

Some say it sailed the Southern seas away from
    winter's cold;
And others say it went a-hunting pirates' hidden
    gold.

Nobody ever saw it but a girl shut in with cough;
She leaned out of her window and she saw it sailing
    off.

From the window of her tenement she waved her
        little hands;
She heard the captain on the bridge call out his
    clear commands.

She said he was a thinnish man, with whitish face
        and wan,
And the name the sailors called him by was Captain
    STEVENSON.

                                    W. L. Werner

"TUSITALA'S" CHRISTENING ODE

Down the bleak, lamp-lit lanes,
Through gusts and squalls of bitter, northern rains,
Strides the figure of a lonely lad, his heart on fire.
Blazing his eyes with passionate desire
For laughter, love and wine, and sunlit France,
Friends — and Romance!
    Uncouth,
In velvet coat and black shirt strangely clad,
Friend of all sad,
Lonely, unhappy youth —
    Tusitala!

    Down by the docks in Brooklyn,
        Where the tides run swift and strong,
    There's a thrill of music in the air
        To the swing of an old sea-song.

For there a tall ship lifts aloft
    Her stately, soaring spars,
And there the ghost of a lonely lad,
    All night beneath the stars,

Treads the deck from stem to stern,
    Dancing with ghostly glee.
"For they call her 'Tusitala'!
    They've named her after me!"

Still down bleak, lamp-lit lanes,
Cursing the rains,
Pass other lads, lonely and sick as he,
Craving romance, laughter, and friends! Yet we,
More fortunate, have him whose name
We cherish as a very flame
That warms, through books, the heart grown sick
    and sad
Of every lonely lad —
    Tusitala!

Down where the salt sea-reaches
    Reëcho the gull's wild cry,
There's a gleaming hull, and the patterned
    spars
    Of a tall ship fill the sky.

O more than ship! For aboard her
    The lonely and friendless find
Laughter — romance — adventure,
    And love, most nobly shrined!

The ghost of a lonely lad looks down,
    And smiles with incredulous glee:

" For they call her 'Tusitala'!
They've named her after me!"

R. D. Turnbull

HAIL—"TUSITALA"!

The following message was written by Joseph Conrad for the *Tusitala*. The MS. is framed in the ship's cabin:

New York, 2nd June, 1923

On leaving this hospitable country, where the cream is excellent and the milk of human kindness apparently never ceases to flow, I assume an ancient mariner's privilege of sending to the owners and the ship's company of the *Tusitala* my brotherly good wishes for fair winds and clear skies on all their voyages. And may they be many!

And I would recommend to them to watch the weather, to keep the halliards clear for running, to remember that "any fool can carry on, but only the wise man knows how to shorten sail" ... and so on, in the manner of ancient mariners all the world over. But the vital truth of sea life is to be found in the ancient saying that it is "the stout hearts that make the ship safe."

Having been brought up on it, I pass it on to them in all confidence and affection.

Joseph Conrad

HOMEWARD BOUND

The lights that gleam along the coast know well our
    passing lights;
The stars that glitter overhead, through countless
    sultry nights

Have watched us trail the same white wake across
    the same dark sea;
Sky, land and ocean lie the same, but newborn men
    are we.

We've touched at every sun-scorched port along
    this blazing shore —
Ceara, Para, Maranho', and others half a score.
We've left four shipmates sleeping 'neath the fever-
    misted ground,
But their loss can't damp our spirits, for tonight
    we're homeward bound!

The hiss of foam beneath the bows, the engine's
    throbbing swing,
Have wearied us for months and yet tonight they
    seem to sing
In harmony a wondrous song: "The time of trial is
    past—
Bahia's lights drop back astern — we're homeward
    bound at last!"

The lookout on the fo'c'sle head, the Black-gang
    down below,
Are singing as the lights glide past and ever north
    we go.
"Four points to port!" The big wheel spins, the
    heavy bows veer round
And straighten out for open sea. Thank God!
    We're homeward bound!

                    William Daniel

THREE TARRY MEN

They came from only God knows where,
Three tarry, blue-eyed men.
They blundered through the swaying train
To empty seats, and then —
Forgotten talk of long ago
I listened to again.

They spoke of rising storm and tides,
Of heaving decks and seas,
Of Port Soudan and Port au Prince,
Seychelles and Hebrides,
Of lonely hours in doldrum calm,
And unsolved mysteries.

Their talk was thick with briny oaths,
And some of it was lies;
They yarned of captains, crews and ships,
Far seas and ports and skies —
But splendid peace and happiness
Shone deep in their blue eyes.

And each one knew, whate'er his talk,
Though cursed as fiend and foe,
The sea was dearer to them all —
And at her word would go
Each mother's son, for none could fail
When she lured, sighing low.

So from the train they lumbered off
With worn and battered grips,

With curses they were leaving port,
But smiles upon their lips,
Down, down the twisting ways to where
There lay the waiting ships.

Edmund Leamy

THE SHIPS

Sing the sea, sing the ships,
Sing the sea and its ships,
With the lightness and the brightness
Of the foam about their lips;
When reaching off to seaward,
When running down to leeward,
When beating up to port with the pilot at the
     fore;
When racing down the Trade,
Or ratching half-afraid,
With a lookout on the yard for the marks along the
     shore.

Sing them when you frame them,
Sing them when you name them,
Sing them as you sing the woman whom you love;
For the world of life they lose you,
For the home that they refuse you,
For the sea that deeps beneath them and the sky
     that crowns above.

Sing them when they leave you,
Sing them when they grieve you,
Going down the harbor with a smoky tug along;
With the yards braced this and that,

And the anchor at the cat,
And the bunting saying "good-bye" to the watch-
    ing, waving throng.

  Sing them when they need you,
  Sing them when they speed you,
With their stems making trouble for the steep
    Atlantic seas;
  When the channel as she rolls
  Heaps the foam along the poles,
And the decks fore-and-aft are awash above your
    knees.

  Sing them when they spring you,
  Sing them when they wing you,
Rolling down the Trades with a breeze that never
    shifts;
  When the crew they quite forget
  What is meant by cold and wet,
And the feel of the braces and the sheets and the
    lifts.

  Sing them when they mock you,
  Sing them when they shock you,
Smothered under topsails with the kingly Horn
    abeam;
  When the wind flies round about
  And the watch is always out,
And all hands are wishing that they'd signed to go
    in steam.

  Sing the sea, sing the ships,
  Sing the sea and its ships,

With the molding and the folding
Of the wave about their form;
Sing them when they teach us,
Sing them when they preach us,
A lesson in the calm and a sermon in the storm.

Sing them when the dying
Wind has left them lying
With the canvas in the brails a-tremble to the rolls;
And the ocean is so still
That you wonder if it will
Give back to her who bore them those legions of
      lost souls.

Sing the sea, sing the ships,
Sing the sea and its ships,
With the forming and the storming
Of the wave athwart their bows;
Sing them when you clear them,
Sing them when you steer them,
For the strength that they have given
And the courage they arouse.

For the nation that forgets them,
For the nation that regrets them,
Is a nation that is dying as the nations all must die;
For there never yet was State
That met the Roman fate
While she had a ship to guard her and a sailor to
      stand by.

For the traffic you have won,
For the web that you have spun,

To catch the flies of commerce and the fleeting
    gnats of trade
  Will be rent and blown away,
  For the weak will never pay
Their earnings to a people who have stamped them-
    selves afraid.

  Pull down the selfish wall!
  We are not cowards all!
There are some who dare to struggle with the
    traders of the world.
  Cast off the nation's chain,
  And give us back the main,
And the flag that's never absent and the sail that's
    never furled.

  Sing the sea, sing the ships,
  Sing the sea and its ships,
  With the mounding and the pounding
  Of the wave along their sides;
  When sailing out and bounding,
  When towing in and rounding,
They drop the anxious anchor and they face the
    swinging tides.

  Sing them when you leave them,
  Sing them when you heave them
To a fast berth, a last berth beside the knackers
    quay;
  For our ships are getting rotten
  And our people have forgotten
The mission of the vessel and the glory of the sea.

Thomas Fleming Day

TOM BOWLING

Here, a sheer hulk, lies poor Tom Bowling,
    The darling of our crew;
No more he'll hear the tempest howling,
    For death has broached him to.
His form was of the manliest beauty,
    His heart was kind and soft;
Faithful below, he did his duty;
    But now he's gone aloft.

Tom never from his word departed,
    His virtues were so rare;
His friends were many and true-hearted;
    His Poll was kind and fair:
And then he'd sing so blithe and jolly,
    Ah, many's the time and oft!
But mirth is turned to melancholy,
    For Tom is gone aloft.

Yet shall poor Tom find pleasant weather,
    When He who all commands,
Shall give, to call Life's crew together,
    The word to "pipe all hands."
Thus Death, who kings and tars despatches,
    In vain Tom's life has doffed;
For, though his body's under hatches,
    His soul is gone aloft.

Charles Dibdin

BILLY PEG-LEG'S FIDDLE

I've a pal called Billy Peg-leg, with one leg a wood
      leg,
And Billy he's a ship's cook and lives upon the
      sea;
And hanging by his griddle
Old Billy keeps a fiddle
For fiddling in the dog-watch
When the moon is on the sea.

We takes our luck wi' tough ships, wi' fast ships,
      wi' free ships,
We takes our luck wi' any ships to slip away to
      sea,
We takes our trick wi' the best o' them
An' sings our song wi' the rest o' them
When the bell strikes for the dog-watch
An' the moon is on the sea.

You'd ought to see the tops'ls, the stuns'ls, the
      stays'ls,
When the moon's a-shinin' on them along a liftin'
      sea;
Hear the dandy bo's'n say:
"Peg-leg, make that fiddle play
An' we'll dance away the dog-watch
While the moon is on the sea."

Then it's fun to watch them dancin', them bow-
      legged sailors dancin',
To the tune o' Peg-leg's fiddle, a-fiddlin' fast an'
      free,

It's fun to watch old Peg-leg
A-waltzin' wi' his wood leg
When bo's'n takes the fiddle
So Peg can dance wi' me.

The moon is on the water, the dark, moon-
    glimmered water,
The night wind pipin' plaintively along a liftin' sea,
There ain't no female wimmen,
No big beer-glasses brimmin',
There's just the great sea's glory
An' Billy Peg an' me.

We takes our luck wi' the tough ship, the tall ship,
    the fast ship,
We takes our luck wi' any ship to sign away for sea,
We takes our trick wi' the best o' them,
An' sings our song wi' the rest o' them,
When the bell strikes for the dog-watch
An' the moon is on the sea.

Bill Adams

THE SAVING OF THE "CORA ANDREWS"

One August day in the early nineties the labor schooner
Cora Andrews put into the port of Kai Island, in the
Louisade Archipelago, with her officers dying of the
plague, and the disease spreading rapidly among the
hundred and twenty blacks which she had recruited in
New Guinea and the Solomons for the Queensland sugar
plantations. A " Captain Bell, beach-comber and habit-
ual drunkard," who is said to have had at one time a com-
mission in the British Navy, while under the influence of
liquor was induced to take the schooner on to Townsville.
This astounding feat the many-times-disgraced officer
successfully accomplished, sailing the schooner for seven

days with no help save that of the plague-stricken blacks,
only to collapse at the wheel when the treacherous Bar-
rier Reef had been safely passed. The story is told by an
old trader of Kai Island.

He piled the gunboat *Firefly* on the Donocaster
      Reef;
At the Motu-Iti Passage his *Molucca* came to grief;
In the pearl lagoon of Happa rests his *Suva* in the
      mud,
And the teeth of Tuka-Tuva ground to dust his
      Flying Scud.

He drowned a hundred niggers in the mouth of
      Torres Strait
Where his brigantine *Brunhilde* rammed the slaver
      Highland Kate:
He lost the *Fakariva* where Levuka's breakers
      roll —
But he saved the *Cora Andrews,* an' perhaps he
      saved his soul.

It was drink — the same old story — that had
      ripped his after leach,
An' dropped him from the Navy to a comber of the
      beach;
But drink it was that won him, 'fore the devil
      claimed his own,
If no seat among the angels, yet some mention
      from the Throne.

The fear of death was on us on that August after-
      noon,
When the slaver *Cora Andrews* dropped her hook in
      Kai Lagoon,

With the air above her hatches reekin' like a rotten
    egg,
An' the skipper, mate an' agent dished and done for
    with the "pleg."

We was fair to goin' crazy when the news spread on
    the beach,
An' no other thought possessed us but to put her
    out o' reach:
An' we met in Jackson's trade-room, an' the dirty
    plot was laid,
With the yells of dyin' niggers driftin' landward on
    the Trade.

Once we got her goin' seaward, she could rot till
    Judgment Day
For all we cared, our one concern was how to get
    her from the bay —
No man, white or black, would touch her, for the
    greatest comber there
Knew to climb the *Cora's* gangway was to mount
    the Golden Stair.
As the thing had nigh to stumped us, when some
    fellow said that Bell,
With a "load," would cram the *Cora* down the
    cracklin' craw o' Hell.
So we sent a nig to fetch him, primed him with a
    drink o' "red,"
Talked, an' worked upon his feelings as the booze
    worked on his head.
Urged him in the name of mercy, cut him with the
    lash of shame;
Flattered him, an' called him plucky — said we
    knew that he was game;

Told him that his soul's redemption hinged upon
    the course he took;
Said he'd get his name recorded in Jehovah's Judg-
    ment Book:
Swore 'twould win him reinstatement in the Navy
    when 'twas found
How he'd took her to Australia — and 'twas this
    that brought him 'round.

No one met his flashin' glances when we sped him
    from the strand,
For we knew death had his tow-line, haulin' in
    hand over hand;
But we watched him, 'shamed an' guilty; saw him
    crack a bottle's neck,
Take a swig, an' then another as he touched the
    quarterdeck.
Saw him set his heavy shoulders, heard the ring of
    sharp command,
Saw the reelin' niggers swarmin' round the capstan
    in a band;
Saw 'em swayin' onto halyards, saw 'em tailin' on a
    sheet,
Heard the bang o' block an' tackle an' the thud o'
    poundin' feet;
Saw 'em raise an' cat the anchor, saw the *Cora* fall
    away
An' go choppin' through the tide-rip at the entrance
    o' the bay.

Seven days Bell sailed the *Cora* from the mouth o'
    Kai Lagoon;
Drove her through a fierce sou'wester, ran her free
    with the Monsoon;

Tossin' over dead in dozens, keepin' up the rest
    with gin;
Cussin', bootin', swearin', breakin' the new sailors
    in.
Day an' night, in ev'ry weather, rampin' wild 'tween
    stem an' stern,
Throwin' down a swig o' whiskey ev'ry time he
    made a turn;
Drivin' on the dyin' niggers, pilin' up the bulgin'
    sail,
Till the *Cora* split the surges, spittin' like a har-
    pooned whale.

Six days out he raised the Barrier — coral shoals
    and coral jaws,
Crooked teeth o' crusted coral, crinkly lines o' coral
    claws —
Damdest piece o' navigation that's in all the Seven
    Seas,
An' Bell took the wheel to steer her, with the
    shakin' o' his knees
And the burnin' o' his gullet, as he downed another
    peg,
Flashin' up as danger signals o' the comin' o' the
    "pleg."

They lashed him to a tripod when his head began to
    reel,
As he hung there, grim, determined, grindin' steady
    at the wheel.
With a parasol an' nigger blockin' off the sun's hot
    rays,
An' a siphon an' a bottle fightin' the eternal blaze.

Seven hours o' steady steerin' — how 'twas done
    defies belief —
An' he'd sailed the *Cora Andrews* safely through
    the Barrier Reef.
They saved some three-score niggers in the Towns-
    ville quarantine,
An' the news o' what had happened brought a cable
    from the Queen;
But the man whose nerve an' courage brought the
    bloomin' *coup* about
Had dropped his own life's anchor as the *Cora's*
    chain ran out.

                  Lewis R. Freeman

THE VOYAGERS

We were weary of our prison, with its wheels that
    grind and roar,
Till we broke the bonds that held us there, and
    knew that we were free,
Till the walls were far behind us and the morning
    star before,
And the life that knows no master and the surging
    of the sea.

So we built a ship and manned her and we left the
    seething town,
And we reached the Northern Ocean where the
    ice-fields heave and groan,
And they fettered us and bound us while the mock-
    ing sun looked down,
And we froze and starved and gloried for the toil
    was all our own.

Then back we came and wearily we sought the
    trodden way,
And we left the ship at anchor and we thought our
    work was done;
Till we looked across the waters and we heard the
    leaping spray
Laugh to scorn our dull contentment in a peace we
    had not won.

So we manned our ship a second time and sailed
    her round the world,
Twenty months of wave and tempest till we
    reached the kindly shore;
Then we brought her back to harbor, once again her
    sails we furled,
And we swore by all the gods of earth to sail the sea
    no more.

But the winds still call us onward to the prize we
    cannot gain,
And rest is dreary to the soul as meadows to the
    eye;
Let us leave the land behind us, let us launch the
    ship again,
And we'll sail for worlds undreamed-of, sail forever
    till we die.

Henry Adams Bellows

THE LAST SHIP

If men who love ships were to choose the last
To be a final vision from the sea —
It would be one of lofty, slender mast

With bright sails filled and lifted gloriously.
It would be such a ship as dreamers knew
By island coast-lines when the dawn was mist
Of stardust and great rubies stricken through
With breakers' foam and bays' tossed amethyst.

It would be a ship that proud adventurers
Rigged up for gold coasts and the pearl lagoon,
And all the dreams they had would yet be hers,
Come in from distant voyages near the moon —
It would be such a ship as makes men sad
With beauty for romance they might have had!

Glenn Ward Dresbach

SEA FEVER

Oh, the sun is striking down at my heart within the
    town,
    And the long streets are leering at my pain;
Will these bells and whistles cease, is there any-
        where there's peace?
    Shall I ever know the wind and spray again?
Give me a boat again, set me out afloat again,
    Sail or keel, oar or wheel, any, anything to feel
Salt and spray upon my face where, lips wet with
        wind, I race,
    Race the clouds and stars again, far from home
        and haunt of men;
For the wind and waterways have stamped me
        with their seal!

Oh, the clamor of the town molds me, holds me
        grimly down,
    And the heat winds its hands about my throat.

But there still is sea somewhere, mist and sea-fog
in the air,
   There are little frail and fairy craft afloat.
Give me an oar again, set me out from shore
again,
   Dark or day, calm or spray, any, anywhere you
say;
Let me feel again the might of the water, let me
fight
   Will to will, strength to strength, hate to hatred,
till at length
Wind and water welcome me, and know me strong
as they!

There is dust and level heat on the black and mov-
ing street,
   And the long night will just repeat the day;
But I'm dreaming of the sea, sail and sea-gull white
and free;
   And I want to drift and listen where they play.
Give me a boat again, set me out afloat again,
   Sail a-shine, white and fine, clouds like whiter
sails in line,
Wave and furrow, spray and foam, this is home and
home and home!
   This is gladness, this is power, this my one tri-
umphant hour!
Leagues of sky, and leagues of sea, and all of it is
mine!

                    Mary Carolyn Davies

D'AVALO'S PRAYER

When the last sea is sailed and the last shallow
 charted,
 When the last field is reaped and the last harvest
 stored,
When the last fire is out and the last guest de-
 parted,
 Grant the last prayer that I shall pray: "Be good
 to me, O Lord!

"And let me pass in a night at sea, a night of storm
 and thunder,
 In the loud crying of the wind through sail and
 rope and spar;
Send me a ninth, great, peaceful wave to drown
 and roll me under
 To the cold tunny-fishes' home where the
 drowned galleons are.

"And in the dim, green, quiet place far out of sight
 and hearing,
 Grant I may hear at whiles the wash and thresh
 of the sea-foam
About the fine, keen bows of the stately clippers
 steering
 Towards the lone northern star and the fair ports
 of home."

John Masefield

PENANG

I want to go back to Singapore
 And ship along the Straits,

To a bungalow I know beside Penang;
    Where cocoanut palms along the shore
        Are waving, and the gates
Of Peace shut Sorrow out forevermore.
    I want to go back and hear the surf
        Come beating in at night,
Like the washing of Eternity over the dead.
    I want to see dawn fare up and day
        Go down in golden light;
I want to go back to Penang! I want to go back!

I want to go back to Singapore
    And up along the Straits,
To the bungalow that waits me by the tide.
    Where the Tamil and Malay tell their lore
        At evening — and the fates
Have set no soothless canker at life's core.
    I want to go back and mend my heart
        Beneath the tropic moon,
While the tamarind-tree is whispering thoughts of
        sleep —
    I want to believe that Earth again
        With Heaven is in tune.
I want to go back to Penang! I want to go back!

I want to go back to Singapore
    And ship along the Straits,
To the bungalow I left upon the strand.
    Where the foam of the world grows faint before
        It enters, and abates
In meaning as I hear the palm-wind pour.
    I want to go back and end my days
        Some evening when the Cross

In the southern sky hangs heavily far and sad.
  I want to remember when I die
      That life elsewhere was loss.
I want to go back to Penang! I want to go back!
                Cale Young Rice

THE TRACKS OF THE TRADES

Take me back, take me back to the Tracks of the
    Trade!
  Let me wander again in the coco palms' shade,
Where the drums of the ocean, in pulsating roar,
  Beat time for the waltz of the waves on the
    shore;
Where sunlight and starlight and moonlight con-
    spire
  To speed the gay hours on the wings of desire;
Let me clamber again through the orchid-bright
    glade —
  Take me back, take me back to the Tracks of the
    Trade!

Oh, the hot flame of sunset, the tremulous light
  When the afterglow fades to the velvet of night!
The star-stencilled headland in blank silhouette
  Where the moonbeams are meshed in the flam-
    boyant's net!
Oh, the purple of midnight, the grey mists of dawn,
  And the amber flood after the darkness has
    gone!
The slow-heaving ocean of gold-spangled jade,
  When the sun wakes the day in the Tracks of the
    Trade!

Let my heart thrill again as the tom-tom's dull
  boom
  Floats out from the bush in the flower-fragrant
    gloom,
And the shriek of the conches, the *hi-mi-ne's* swell,
  Brings word of the feast in the depths of the
    dell.
Lead my footsteps again to that forest-crypt dim,
  Where the firelight throws shadows on bosom
    and limb,
Of the billowing forms of the trim tropic-maids,
  When the song wakes the dance in the Tracks of
    the Trades!

Let my hands close again on the hard-kicking
  wheel,
  As the schooner romps off on a rollicking reel,
To the humming of back-stay and sharp-slatting
  sail,
  And the hiss of the comber that smothers the
    rail.
Oh, the cadenced lament of the chorusing shroud,
  As the spindrift sweeps aft in a feathery cloud!
Oh, the storm-tumbled sea-ways traversed un-
  afraid,
  As the squalls spin the spume down the Tracks
    of the Trade!

Take me back, take me back to the Tracks of the
  Trade!
  For 'tis weary I am of the city's parade,
Of the dust of the traffic, the grey, cheerless skies,
  And the long lines of people with spiritless eyes.

Take me back to my green, sunny islands again,
  Away from this treadmill of sorrow and pain,
Away from this tinsel and gilt masquerade —
  Let me live, let me die in the Tracks of the
      Trade!

Lewis R. Freeman

THE SEAFARER

Shanghaied in San Francisco,
We brought up in Bombay
Where they put us afloat an old Leith boat
That steered like a stack of hay.

We've sweltered in the Tropics
When the pitch boiled through the deck —
And saved our hides and little besides
In an ice-cold North Sea wreck.

We've drunk our rum in Portland
And we've thrashed through Bering Strait —
And we've toed the mark on a Yankee barque
With a hard-case Down-east mate.

We know the streets of Santos
And the loom of the lone Azores —
We've eat our grub from a salt-horse tub
Condemned from the Navy stores.

We know the quay of Glasgow
And the river at Saigon —
We've drunk our glass with a Chinese lass
In a house-boat at Canton.

We know the road to Auckland
And the light on Sydney Head —
And we've crept close-hauled when the leads-
    man called
The depth of the Channel bed.

They pay us off in London
And it's "O for a spell ashore!"
But again we ship for the Southern trip
In a week or hardly more.

For — it's "Goodbye Sally and Sue"
And — "It's time to get afloat —",
With an aching head and a straw-stuffed bed,
And a knife and an oil-skin coat.

Sing — "Time to leave her, Johnny!"
Sing — "Bound for the Rio Grande!"
When the tug turns back you follow her track
For a last, long look at land.

Then the purple disappears —
And only the blue is seen —
That will take our bones to Davy Jones
And our souls to Fiddler's Green.

Anonymous

A TIME-EXPIRED MAN

I coaled the ship and I scrubbed down decks,
    And I worked like an army mule —
For the outfit isn't a dress parade;
    It's a hard and bitter school;

They gave me the steel of the stabbin' word,
  And the weight of the iron han';
They gave me the gaff of the belt and boot —
  But they drilled me into a man.

They put me into the training-school
  Before they gave me my blues;
They taught me to drill and to scrub my clothes,
  Then they sent me out on a cruise;
They taught me to read and write and spell,
  And to handle a twelve-inch gun;
I learned my lesson and learned it well —
  And it wasn't all of it fun.

I didn't learn much of the Golden Rule
  And I didn't learn much about prayer,
But I learned the iron Rules of the Game
  Where they play it on the Square;
I learned a lot that's not down in the Book
  Afloat on the naked spray —
For the sea puts fear in the boldest hearts
  And grit in the meanest clay.

I've cruised in the far Alaska seas
  Where the iron-shod icebergs churn;
I've stood my watch 'neath the Southern Cross
  With the waves afire astern;
I've sweltered on Guantanamo beach
  For full six months in the sheer,
With never the sight of a woman's face
  Nor the smell of gin or beer.

I've been in the House of the Thousand Steps
  In the land of the Japanee,

Takin' my tea with a Geisha Girl —
　　And I've been upon the spree
At the God-forsaken ends of the earth
　　With a God-forsaken crew,
And I've done all the God-forsaken things
　　That a sailor-man will do.

I've learned to polish the bright-work clean
　　As the face of a mission saint,
And I've learned to look on the sight of blood
　　Without turnin' sick and faint;
I've rolled the bones and I've turned the cards,
　　And I've taken my pay-day swig;
I've broken Shore-liberty once or twice,
　　And I've done my time in the brig.

I've done my share of hoppin' about
　　With the girls on Avon Street,
And they're the devil's own pirate-crew —
　　But on one I was passin' sweet.
And now it's all over and put behind,
　　And I'm a civilian once more —
But I can't forget and I won't forget
　　Tho' I'm anchored snug a-shore.

I coaled the ship and I scrubbed down decks
　　And I worked like an army mule —
For the outfit isn't a dress parade —
　　It's a hard and bitter school;
They gave me the steel of the stabbin' word,
　　And the weight of the iron han';
They gave me the gaff of the belt and boot —
　　But they drilled me into a man.
　　　　　　　　　　John G. Gartland

THE REEFS

(Isles of Scilly)

Who sank the "Primo"?
"I," said the Seven Stones,
"And then ate her bones.
She crashed bows on with her sails in tatters,
I broke her up as a mallet shatters
An egg. She didn't take long to vanish.
I heard her people praying in Spanish
In the boiling lather of surf that draped me,
And only a single dago escaped me—
       I sank the 'Primo.'"

Who sank the "Sussex"?
"I," said the Seal,
"I ripped up her keel.
She came from Baltimore carrying cattle,
And oh but I laughed to see 'em battle
For shore, the blockheads, mooing and blowing,
With whirlpools sucking and currents towing
Them back. They sank where the grey rock
           cod is;
The sea was thick with their drifting bodies—
       I sank the 'Sussex.'"

Who sank the "Association"?
"I," said the Gilstone,
"She sank like a millstone.
A ship o' the line, a huge first-rater;
I sank the 'Eagle' and 'Romney' later.
The cabin-boy, who was born in a hovel,
Lord High Admiral Cloudesley Shovel,

Him I drowned, and his captains 'round him,
A woman buried him where she found him,
Out on the sands with the sea-birds wailing,
A Lord High Admiral home from sailing —
    I sank the 'Association.'"

    Who sank the "Schiller"?
    "I," said Re-tarrier,
    "She challenged my barrier.
As big as a church and as tall as a steeple,
Crammed with specie and mails and people,
Into my jaws the night-fogs drove her,
She struck, and crumpled, and then heeled over.
Her boats were swamped as she rolled and crushed
    them,
The women shrieked till the black seas hushed
    them.
I drowned three hundred as easy as winking,
Which wasn't a bad night's work I'm thinking —
    I sank the 'Schiller.'"

Then the grim rocks that stand guard about
    Scilly —
Buccaboo, Great Smith, and Little Granilly,
The Barrel of Butter, Dropnose and Hellweather —
Started to boast of their conquests together,
Of drowned men and gallant tall vessels laid
    low,
While gulls wheeled about them like flurries of
    snow,
And green combers romped at them smashing in
    thunder,
Gurgling and booming in caverns down under,

Sending their diamond drops flying in showers.
"Oh!" said the reefs, "What a business is ours!
Since saints in coracles paddled from Erin
(Fishing our waters for sinners and herrin'),
And purple-sailed triremes of Hamilcar came
To the Islands of Tin, we've played at the game.
We shattered the galleys of conquering Rome,
The galleons of Philip, that scudded for home,
(The sea-molluscs' slime on their glittering gear),
We plundered the plundering French privateer.
We caught the great Indiaman head in the wind,
And gutted her hold of the treasures of Ind;
We broke the proud ships of His Majesty's fleet
(The bones of their seamen lie bleached at our
　　feet),
And cloudy tea-clippers that raced from Canton,
Swept into our clutches — and never went on.
Came steel leviathans mocking disaster,
We scrapped them as fast — if anything faster.
So pick up your pilot and take a cross-bearing,
Sound us and chart us from Lion to Tearing,
And ring us with light-houses, day-marks and
　　buoys,
The gales are our hunters, the fogs our decoys.
We shall not go hungry; we grin, and we wait,
Black-fanged and foam-drabbled, the wolves at the
　　gate."

Crosbie Garstin

TAKEN SHIP

Tonight, about the little town
　　The lights will glimmer, golden soft;

But I shall be horizon-down
　　Facing the stars that climb aloft.

And you, tonight, around the fire,
　　Will draw the curtains, pitying me;
When I have found my heart's desire —
　　The wide wind and the swinging sea!

Charles Buxton Going

WINDOWS OVER WATER

Over the harbor, now, the gulls go keening —
　　Flakes of translated foam against the blue;
Along the wind a lone white sail is leaning:
　　There will be fog before the fishing's through.

How should I care what boat returns well
　　　　freighted —
　　Who minds a helm or keeps the tackle clear?
What odds to me if early or belated,
　　Safe sheltered from the Sea's old mischief here?

The dark pines drip; the gulls have ceased their
　　　　crying;
　　The surf, like some ironic titan, mocks
Our trivial ways of living and of dying;
　　Driftwood piles up among the jagged rocks.

Grayness above me, and a gray mist under,
　　And in my heart a thing I cannot say . . .
Why should I lie awake tonight and wonder
　　How many boats are anchored in the bay?

Leslie Nelson Jennings

CEYLON

I hear a whisper in the heated air —
"Rest! Rest! give over care!"
Long, level breakers on the golden beach
Murmur in silver speech —
"Sleep in the palm-tree shadows on the
  shore —
Work, work no more!
Rest here and work no more."

Where half unburied cities of dead kings
Breed poisonous creeping things
I learn the poor mortality of man —
Seek vainly for some plan —
Know that great empires pass as I must pass
Like withered blades of grass —
Dead blades of Patna grass.

"Breathe — breathe the odorous sweetness that
  is ours,"
Cry Frangipani flowers.
"Forget! Forget! and know no more distress,
But languorous idleness:
Dream where dead leaves fall ever from green
  trees
To float on sapphire seas —
Dream! and be one with these."

      A. Hugh Fisher

THE LAST HARBOR

Now the men who shipped aboard of me in other
    days were these:
Andy Mack of Gloucester, Hernandeau from
    Quebec,
And "Freshwater" Kilmanton, and "Salt Sam"
    Peck,
And skipper Byce and young Byce who walked the
    after deck.
But they're gone, and I lie listening to old voices
    from the seas.

And sun-rotting at a dock is no decent death to
    die!
If tides would lift me high enough, and rotten ropes
    would break,
I'd run a last, high, windy course for old time's
    sake;
Old hands upon my tiller and new foam in my
    wake,
Out where white-rimmed water hills race to meet
    the sky.

Lifted on the crest of them, I'd face the yellow
    sun,
And racing down their farther slopes, I'd plunge
    through foaming green,
Sinking slow, unbroken, like a stately-stepping
    queen,
Down to still, dark waters the sun has never seen,
And never ship may find them till her last voyage
    is done.

Andy Mack's at rest out there, a hundred fathom
    down,
And young Byce is with him, and they'd cheer to
    see me ride
Past the reach of hungry waves, below the lowest
    tide,
Into some green, weedy harbor of the deep sea's
    under side,
Where the Lord gives peace to sailor men and good
    ships when they drown!

Helen Ives Gilchrist

A BURIAL AT SEA

And one of the missionary women thought
That there wasn't much to be said for the dead
    man,
Since he was a Hindu and a Heathen.
Meanwhile,
A sailor sewed him up in canvas —
Like a Christian or a Turk, or any one else.
And we rigged a platform out of dunnage
From the number two hatch to the rail,
And had a plank ready to balance the body on.
At six bells the crew was mustered forward.
The passengers looked on from the bridge deck,
While a Wisconsin missionary, in a blue serge
    suit,
Read the burial service for the dead.
And we all bowed stiffly as he led in prayer,
With the hot sun stinging on our bended necks.
"Thine is the Kingdom and the Power —"
Repeated here and there in a voice like the rattle

Of a heel block under the winch's fall;
"And the Glory for Ever and Ever. Amen."
Then we stretched a new British flag
Over the canvas on the balanced plank,
The skipper called to the officer on the bridge,
"Give them slow bell in the engine room."
The telegraph rattled. And the ship began to
     roll
Heavily and slow as she lost headway.
"Ashes . . . Dust . . . let him be thrown into the
     sea."
Chips raised one end of the plank,
And the body slid away
From under the shelter of the flag,
And out of human keeping —
Splash!
The telegraph rattled once more,
And the ship began to steady under way.
The passengers all talked.
The Bos'n's gang went back to chipping rust.
The quartermaster at the wheel
Struck seven bells in pairs, with the odd one
Left over for the hour.
A lady went by, wiping her eyes on a handker-
     chief,
And the missionary from Wisconsin paused to
     bewail
The cheapness of life in the East,
While an ape-like Filipino boy
Argued that Hindus are a kind of monkey —
Not to be classed as human.

                 A. Binns

OUT OF THE FOG

Out of the fog Death rode with great, still bows;
　Then ship met ship with horrid agony —
Steel locked and broke ... the bloodied faces
　　stared
　With sudden understanding at the sea.

All movement ceased; the world was sick and
　　still —
　Then footsteps beat the buckled deck, and cries
Began ... and all the humanness was gone,
　And light and life were little vanished lies.

And there were women — futile, precious things;
　And round-faced babies that they clutched and
　　kissed,
And tearing wood, and the white name of God,
　And dead men dropping blackly through the mist.

Then through that hell a lad stood smiling, calm:
　"Here, ma'am ... take my belt ... Hurry now
　　... Good-by."
Came the last shudder of the broken ship —
　And Youth once more had taught us how to die!
Dana Burnet

THE WARD ROOM TOAST

Sweethearts and wives — girls that we left behind,
　Blue eyes and brown — dim when we sailed that
　　day;
For Jack at sea do they grow soft and kind,
　May memories come to keep the tears away.

Beneath strange suns we've sailed the Seven Seas,
  Where woman's glance the Yankee sailor lures;
Our flag has fluttered in the Orient breeze,
  But never have we met with eyes like yours.

Sweethearts and wives — speeding across the sky
  We send our longing message — "Here's to
    you,"
The girls we love — the gallant flag we fly —
  The hearts that tremble for the boys in blue.

See — clear a beacon glows beyond the foam,
  Steady and warm its welcome never dies;
Ah, keep it burning for us there at home,
  The sailor's star — the lovelight in your eyes!

Now — once again, boys — steady there — stand
    by!
  A glass with you, sir — now then — three times
    three!
"The Stars and Stripes forever! Bumpers dry —
  Our flag — our ship — our hearts across the sea!"
                                        Anonymous

SEALED ORDERS

From the Golden Gate where the sunsets wait,
Through the smooth Pacific seas,
While the day grows dim, in our war paint grim,
On our beam the orange trees.
By light after light, through the soundless night,
Past cape and headland drear,

While the shaded light, from the binnacle bright,
Shows the compass card swing clear.
   "East, south-east!"
     "Aye, Aye, Sir! East, south-east!"

O'er the tropic seas, when the faint land-breeze,
Scarce stirs the awnings, spread,
When the hand-rails burn, and the wake astern,
Seems cut in a sea of lead.
When the men drop fast, to the fire-hold's blast,
And a watch seems a thousand years,
To her course held true — to sky-line blue
Still onward our vessel steers.
   "South, half-west!"
     "Aye, Aye, Sir! South, half-west!"

There is ice in the air, and our decks are bare,
While the bridge is white with spray.
But there's work to do, so our wheel's held true,
And our twin guns point the way.
Under battened hatch, our engines match
Their might to the "blind Horn's" wrath
While, to port, on the shore, the breakers roar
As we speed on our ocean path.
   "East — nor'-east!"
     "Aye, Aye, Sir! East — nor'-east!"

There's a message hid by the big oak lid,
Of the Captain's desk, locked fast,
But the good news grows and the cook's-mate
     knows
There's a fight in sight, at last.

With a " full-speed " bell — our engines tell
Of their interest in the news,
And the dishes crack, in the mess-room rack
With the jar of the whirling screws.
    "Nor'-west-by-west!"
      "Aye, Aye, Sir! Nor'-west-by-west!"

Now the fleet is nigh, and our flag on high,
With a roar from the signal gun.
To her place on the right, all fit for fight,
And a cheer from them — every one.
The long trip's past and the flags speak fast
And West greets East once more.
'Tis a record trip of a Yankee ship
As it was in the days of yore.
    "Anchor's clear! Sir!"
      "Very good! Let go!"

Oregon Signals.
    "Did you save me a place in the line, Sisters?
    I have travelled afar for this sign,
    When the guns speak plain, for our sister Maine,
    Did you save me a place in the line?"

Flag-ship Answers.
    "All together in thunders loud, Sister!
    We will talk through our open ports
    Till Blanco's brag and the Spanish flag
    Go down with the Morro forts."
      "Two thousand and fifty yards!" "Fire!"
                      E. E. C. Gibbs

THE RUSH OF THE "OREGON"

They held her South to Magellan's mouth,
  Then East they steered her forth
Through the farther gate of the crafty strait,
  And then they held her North.

Six thousand miles to the Indian Isles!
  And the *Oregon* rushed home,
Her wake a swirl of jade and pearl,
  Her bow a bend of foam.

And when at Rio the cable sang,
  "There is war!— grim war with Spain!"
The swart crews grinned and stroked their guns
  And thought on the mangled *Maine*.

In the glimmering gloom of the engine room
  There was joy to each grimy soul,
And fainting men sprang up again
  And piled the blazing coal.

Good need was there to go with care;
  But every sailor prayed
Or gun for gun, or six to one,
  To meet them, unafraid.

Her goal at last! With joyous blast
  She hailed the welcoming roar
Of hungry sea-wolves curved along
  The strong-hilled Cuban shore.

Long nights went by. Her beaмèd eye,
  Unwavering, searched the bay

Where trapped and penned for a certain end
  The Spanish squadron lay.

Out of the harbor a curl of smoke —
  A watchful gun rang clear.
Out of the channel the squadron broke
  Like a bevy of frightened deer.

Then there was shouting for "Steam, more
      steam!"
  And the fires gleamed white and red;
And guns were manned, and ranges planned,
  And the great ships leaped ahead.

Then there was roaring of chorusing guns,
  Shatter of shell, and spray;
And who but the *Oregon*
  Was fiercest in chase and fray!

For her mighty wake was a seething snake;
  Her bow was a billow of foam;
Like the mailèd fists of an angry wight
  Her shot drove crashing home!

Pride of the Spanish navy, Ho!
  Flee like a hounded beast!
For the Ship of the Northwest strikes a blow
  For the Ship of the far Northeast!

In quivering joy she surged ahead,
  Aflame with flashing bars,
Till down sunk the Spaniard's gold and red
  And up ran the Clustered Stars.

"Glory to share?" Aye, and to spare;
  But the chiefest is her's by right
Of a rush of fourteen thousand miles
  For the chance of a bitter fight!

Arthur Guiterman

REALIZATION

When I was a lad, I used to read
  By Summer afternoons and nights,
Of adventurers in square-rigged ships,
  Of foreign ports and splendid sights.

And I would dream upon the day,
  When I should know a heaving deck,
Or beach a long-boat on the sand,
  Beside some buried galleon-wreck.

Now I am gone to see the world;
  Nor all the eager dreams of youth,
Afire with tale of pirate gold,
  Have conjured up the living truth.

The odor of the water-fronts,
  The sun-white sand of coral keys;
No tale of verse may ever hint
  One-half the spell of far, deep seas.

Ira South

SEA BORN

My mother bore me in an island town,
  So I love windy water and the sight
Of luggers sailing by in thin moonlight, —
  I wear the sea as others wear a crown.

My mother bore me near the spinning water,
　　Water was the first sound upon my ears,
And near the sea her mother bore her daughter,
　　Close to a window looking on the weirs.

Ever a wind is moaning where I go,
　　I never stand at night upon a quay,
But I must strain my eyes for sails that blow,
　　But I must strain my ears to hear the sea.
My mother bore me in an island town —,
　　I wear the sea as others wear a crown.

Harold Vinal

THE COASTERS

Overloaded, undermanned,
　　Trusting to a lee,
Playing I-spy with the land,
　　Jockeying the sea —
That's the way the Coaster goes,
　　Through calm and hurricane:
Everywhere the tide flows,
Everywhere the wind blows,
　　From Mexico to Maine.

O East and West! O North and South!
　　We ply along the shore,
From famous Fundy's foggy mouth,
　　From voes of Labrador;
Through pass and strait, on sound and sea,
　　From port to port we stand —
The rocks of Race fade on our lee,
　　We hail the Rio Grande.

Our sails are never lost to sight;
    On every gulf and bay
They gleam, in winter wind-cloud white,
    In summer rain-cloud gray.

We hold the coast with slippery grip;
    We dare from cape to cape;
Our leaden fingers feel the dip
    And trace the channel's shape.
We sail or bide as serves the tide —
    Inshore we cheat its flow,
And side by side at anchor ride
    When stormy head-winds blow.
We are the offspring of the shoal,
    The hucksters of the sea;
From customs' theft and pilot toll
    Thank God that we are free.

Legging on and off the beach,
    Drifting up the strait,
Fluking down the river reach,
    Towing through the gate —
That's the way the Coaster goes,
    Flirting with the gale:
Everywhere the tide flows,
Everywhere the wind blows,
    From York to Beavertail.

Here and there to get a load,
    Freighting anything;
Running off with spanker stowed,
    Loafing wing-a-wing —

That's the way the Coaster goes,
　　Chumming with the land:
Everywhere the tide flows,
Everywhere the wind blows,
　　From Ray to Rio Grande.

We split the swell where rings the bell
　　On many a shallow's edge,
We take our flight past many a light
　　That guards the deadly ledge;
We greet Montauk across the foam,
　　We work the Vineyard Sound,
The Diamond sees us running home,
　　The Georges outward bound;
Absecon hears our canvas beat
　　When tacked off Brigantine;
We raise the Gulls with lifted sheet,
　　Pass wing-and-wing between.

Off Monomoy we fight the gale,
　　We drift off Sandy Key;
The watch of Fenwick sees our sail
　　Scud for Henlopen's lee,
With decks awash and canvas torn
　　We wallow up the Stream;
We drag dismasted, cargo borne,
　　And fright the ships of steam.
Death grips us with his frosty hands
　　In calm and hurricane;
We spill our bones on fifty sands
　　From Mexico to Maine.

Cargo reef in main and fore,
　　Manned by half a crew,

Romping up the weather shore,
Edging down the Blue —
That's the way the Coaster goes,
Scouting with the lead:
Everywhere the tide flows,
Everywhere the wind blows,
From Cruz to Quoddy Head.

Thomas Fleming Day

THE WOOLEY

Talk as you please of a scrap with a Hun
Caught like a rat in a corner,
If you are looking for trouble, not fun,
Sail on an old Cape Horner
Or, better, a South Pole whaler, lad,
And face the wind where the wind runs mad.

A cornered Hun is no more than a man,
And the better man will lick him;
But the wind, old when the world began,
Could tackle old Ned and trick him;
And of all foul winds the Wooley's the worst,
Of a black sky born, by a milk-sea nursed.

It will come so quick and'll lam so hard,
All's over before you've started;
It will catch the cagiest off his guard,
Put crimps in the stoutest-hearted:
It isn't a thing you can fight with a gun,
Bayonet, knife or your fists, my son.

Richard Butler Glaenzer

THE PIRATES OF TORTUGA

I

Pierre le Grand has one blind eye,
And fingers eight are Pierre's,
But the stoutest blades in Carib seas
Come when he pipes to prayers.
And the buzzards swinging round the poop
They shiver when he swears.

We were eight and twenty men
On a Carib cockleshell,
Eight and twenty cursing pirates
Broiling on the tropic swell.

Not a breath o' wind above us,
Not a pint o' rum inside —
And the salt-pork like a razor
Pulling at a blistered hide.

Quoth Portúgues, "In Tortuga,
Cool an' quiet by the quay,
There's a crowd o' pirates settin'
Round a barrel by a tree.

"And the yarns is good an' juicy
And the rum is redder'n fire,
And the wind strums on the palm-tops
Like a angel on a lyre."

Quoth Black Barley, "In Tortuga
There is girls of every shade,
And they're splashin' in the surf now,
Fair and bare as they was made.

"And they's white an' black an' copper —
  And they glistens every one
Like an ingot, like a hell-bent
  Bloody ingot in the sun."

Sighs old Benjam, "In Tortuga
  I've a wife as pert as they.
And I'd give my eye to know just
  How she whiles the hours away."

*"There'll be pirates in Tortuga
  That can tell you when we land."*
"Lies!" — *"A knife!"* — "Knives are for
      Spaniards!
  Put 'em up!" cries Pierre le Grand.

"We're but eight and twenty men,
  And I'll have no lifted hand
Till a galleon bound for Cadiz
  Tops the west," quoth Pierre le Grand.

Cries Black Barley, "Galleons, galleons!
  Forty days and nights we stew.
Jesus! What a laugh Tortuga'll
  Laugh, at this boiled pirate-crew!"

Pierre le Grand, the lifeless tiller
  Clutched. His scars shot purple-red.
"You'll not hear the laugh. Tortuga'll
  See you either rich or dead."

II

Like a red *Carolus Quintus*
  Over Cuba sank the sun,

But its last ray struck the Cross, high
  On a Spanish galleon—

We were eight and twenty men,
  And we plied the oars like whips.
And Pierre he hugged the tiller
  With a black smile on his lips.

And the night grew thick, and heavy
  As a gravecloth drooped the air.
And the sea-fires lit our faces
  With a green and ghostly flare.

Cries Portúgues, "Sou'-sou' westward
  Burns a light!" And Pierre: "Speak low!
Swine o' Satan!" Like a serpent,
  Crawling on a bird, we go.

Sou'-sou' westward like a great bird
  Tangled in a web of stars
On the oily swell the galleon
  Dips her black and lazy spars.

From the middle poop-deck glimmers
  Dim the cabin-lamp, and hark!
Comes a crazy, clear fandango
  With a laugh across the dark.

And the man beside me shivers,
  And I shiver as we skulk
Like a cat across the waters
  Toward that awful, dreaming hulk.

But Pierre le Grand scowls whitely
   From his narrow, restless eye.
"Scuttle ship! We make Tortuga
   In a galleon, or we die."

And the surgeon's clotted bone-saw
   Like a rat gnaws at the planks.
And the waters, black and hungry,
   Gurgle their triumphant thanks.

With the tiller 'neath his armpit,
   And a pistol in each hand,
Cold and silent by the galleon's
   Heavy prow waits Pierre le Grand.

From the black poop through the blackness —
   God, we held our breath — a cry!
"Sixes, damn you!" "Tierces!" "Sixes!"
   "Put your blade up!" — "Let me by!"

Shouts and falling chairs, a moan!
   Silence. Then a low command.
"Up the forestay! Up and over!"
   And the first was Pierre le Grand.

At the prow a lousy Spaniard
   Stirred. "Quick, choke him!" That man died.
Then by sail and rail, like panthers!
   And Pierre le Grand was guide.

We were eight and twenty men,
   And we stepped like careful ghosts.

Itching foot and itching cutlass,
    Through those black and snoring hosts.

Down the waist and up the gangways!
    By an open door we stand.
Once more comes the cursing laughter —
    "I go first," said Pierre le Grand.

Tiptoe down the reeking passage —
    Then a great carved door, ajar —
And we stand with grinning faces
    Where the drunk hidalgos are.

Six men sprawling over dice-cups,
    And they turned not hand nor head.
And the only man that saw us
    Lay beside a divan, dead.

Not a sound. The dices' rattle
    Only, and an oath, half choked;
While the candle to the low beams
    Sputtered, flared and wildly smoked.

Tiptoe, and behind each Spaniard
    Soft, a pirate took his stand
Like a Memnon out of Egypt —
    And the first was Pierre le Grand.

"Cinq and deuce! one throw more! Sixes!
    Back, ye sucklings, to Peru!
Farthings, ducats, guineas, ingots!"
    And his drunken head he threw

Backwards, chuckling golden triumph —
  Gurgled, stared — *"Christ! Devils!"* then
Silence, a quenched candle, darkness —
  And the gasps of choking men.

"Devils!" "Ay!" laughed Pierre. *"Have mercy!"*
  "First I'll have your ship and gold,
Farthings, ducats, guineas, ingots,
  And what else burns in your hold."

And Pierre le Grand glared hotly
  From his fierce and bloodshot eye,
"Bind, gag! And the round half dozen
  Throttle, if one makes a cry!"

Then, a whispered word, and softly
  Twenty pirates at his beck
Tiptoed down the reeking passage
  To the noisy slumber-deck;

Crouched, and watched like heavenly angels
  O'er the blesséd, till the day
Broke, and sullenly the sailors
  Turned their ship Tortuga-way.

III

In Tortuga there were stirrings
  When we loomed against the east —
Tumult and wild shouts: "The Spaniard
  Comes to murder and to feast!"

And they hid their gems and bullion,
  Pushed wide many a secret panel —

Set a score of guns a-gaping
   O'er the narrow harbor-channel.

Boom! Across our bows a cannon
   Splashed its challenge in the bay.
But before an hour, Tortuga
   Greeted us a better way.

For the Bishop blest our coming
   And the Governor shed tears,
And the girls danced round and loved us
   With new jewels in their ears.

Ten swift days and nights Tortuga
   Was a mad and dizzy land,
Save for one man counting ducats
   On his galleon — Pierre le Grand.

Eight and twenty shining mountains
   From the glowing casks he told.
And the tenth night a crazed pirate
   Stabbed and killed him o'er his gold.

Hermann Hagedorn

PORTS OF CALL

All around the world they lie,
   On all the forty seas,
And the chorus of their call goes by
   On every vagrant breeze;
Sleepy little beach towns,
   A-sprawl for miles and miles,
Or dirty river-reach towns,
   On delta mud and piles.

Barrios and Santos,
    Sydney, Loango,
Nagasaki, Saigon,
    Colon and Callao —
Their names are siren music
    To make you want to go.

Oh, they'll never let a man be good,
    They whisper in his ear,
Until the fever heats his blood
    To see the big ships clear.
They call ever to the rover,
    They sing of steam and sail:
"Come out and look us over;
    Get up and hit the trail!"

Constant and Aleck,
    Smyrna, Tripoli,
Sandakan, Shanghai,
    Cadiz-by-the-sea —
Oh, the finest hymn-book printed
    Is an old geography!

Leo Hays

O, FALMOUTH IS A FINE TOWN

O, Falmouth is a fine town with ships in the bay,
And I wish from my heart it's there I was to-day;
I wish from my heart I was far away from here,
Sitting in my parlor and talking to my dear.
For it's home, dearie, home — it's home I want to
        be.
Our topsails are hoisted, and we'll away to sea.

O, the oak and the ash and the bonnie birken
    tree,
They're all growing green in the old countrie.

In Baltimore a-walking a lady I did meet
With her babe on her arm as she came down the
    street;
And I thought how I sailed, and the cradle standing
    ready
For the pretty little babe that has never seen its
    daddie.
    And it's home, dearie, home, —

O, if it be a lass, she shall wear a golden ring;
And if it be a lad, he shall fight for his king;
With his dirk and his hat and his little jacket
    blue
He shall walk the quarter-deck as his daddie used
    to do.
    And it's home, dearie, home, —

O, there's a wind a-blowing, a-blowing from the
    west,
And that of all the winds is the one I like the best,
For it blows at our backs, and it shakes our pennon
    free,
And it soon will blow us home to the old countrie.
For it's home, dearie, home — it's home I want to
    be.
Our topsails are hoisted, and we'll away to sea.
O, the oak and the ash and the bonnie birken tree,
They're all growing green in the old countrie.
                                        William E. Henley

MERCHANDISE

Merchandise! Merchandise! Tortoise-shell,
    spices,
Carpets and indigo — sent o'er the high seas;
Mother-o'-pearl from the Solomon Isles —
Brought by a brigantine ten thousand miles.
Rubber from Zanzibar, tea from Nang-Po,
Copra from Hayti, and wine from Bordeaux;
Ships, with top-gallants and royals unfurled,
Are bringing in freights from the ends of the
    world.

Crazy old wind-jammers, manned by Malays,
With rat-ridden bulkheads and creaking old stays,
Reeking of bilge and of paint and of pitch —
That's how your fat city merchant grew rich.
But with " tramps," heavy laden, and liners untold
You may lease a new life to a world that's grown
    old.
Merchandise! Merchandise! Nations are made
By their men and their ships and their overseas
    trade.

So widen your harbors, your docks and your quays,
And hazard your wares on the wide ocean ways,
Run out your railways and hew out your coal,
For only by trade can a country keep whole.
Feed up your furnaces, fashion your steel,
Stick to your bargains and pay on the deal;
Rich is your birthright, and well you'll be paid
If you keep in good faith with your overseas
    trade.

Learn up geography — work out your sums,
Build up your commerce, and pull down your slums;
Sail on a Plimsoll that marks a full hold —
Your overseas trade means a harvest of gold.
Bring in the palm-oil and pepper you've bought,
But send out ten times the amount you import;
Trade your inventions, your labor and sweat —
Your overseas traffic will keep ye from debt.

Hark to the song of the shuttle and loom,
"Keep up your commerce or crawl to your tomb!"
Study new methods and open new lines,
Quicken your factories, foundries and mines.
Think of Columbus, De Gama and Howe,
And waste not their labors by "slacking it" now;
Work is life's currency — earn what you're worth,
And send out your ships to the ends of the earth.

For deep-bosomed mothers with wide-fashioned
        hips
Will bear ye good sons for the building of ships;
Good sons for your ships and good ships for your
        trade —
That's how the peace of the world will be made!
So, send out your strong to the forests untrod,
Work for yourselves and your neighbors and God;
Keep these great nations the homes of the free,
With merchandise, men and good ships on the sea.
Merchandise! Merchandise! Good, honest mer-
        chandise!
Merchandise, men and good ships on the sea.
                                        Anonymous

THE LAST VOYAGE

When I loose my vessel's moorings, and put out to
      sea once more
On the last and longest voyage that shall never
      reach the shore,
O Thou Master of the Ocean, send no tranquil tides
      to me,
But 'mid all Thy floods and thunders let my vessel
      put to sea.

Let her lie within no tropic sea, dead rotten to the
      bone,
Till the lisping, sluggish waters claim my vessel for
      their own;
Till the sun shall scar her timbers, and the slimy
      weed shall crawl
O'er her planks that gape and widen, and the slow
      sea swallow all.

Let her not go down in darkness, where the smok-
      ing mist-wreaths hide
The white signal of the breakers, dimly guessed at,
      overside;
While her decks are in confusion, and the wreck
      drops momently,
And she drifts in dark and panic to the death she
      cannot see.

But out in the open ocean, where the great waves
      call and cry,
Leap and thunder at her taffrail, while the scud
      blows stinging by,

With the life still strong within her, struggling on-
    ward through the blast,
Till one last, long wave shall whelm her, and our
    voyaging is past.

Norah M. Holland

RIVER BOATS

The boats upon the river
  Speak ever to my heart;
And whether they drag anchor,
  Impatient to depart,
Or whether they ply inland,
  Or turn them to the sea,
No two of them are calling
  In any selfsame key.
For mighty ocean liners
  Let forth a slow, deep blast,
While tugs, black-browed and stodgy,
  Pipe sharp and shrill and fast,
And battered tropic steamers
  Vouchsafe a few hoarse notes:
There's magic in the whistle
  Of all the river boats.
And yet although my pulses
  Acclaim each separate voice,
The ship above all others
  That leads me to rejoice
Is one whose sails to breezes
  Are lithely, mutely flung:
The brigantine, the schooner —
  The ship without a tongue.

Anonymous

THE TANKERS

To Bombay and Capetown, and ports of a hundred
    lands,
To Mombasa, Panama, and Aden-on-the-sands,
Red with rust and green with mold, caked with
    sodden brine,
The reeling, rolling tankers sail southward from the
    Tyne.

Southward past the Cornish cliffs, cleft red against
    the clouds,
They snort and stagger onward with sailors in their
    shrouds,
To the spell of rolling seas and the blue of a windy
    sky,
While the smoke lies brown to leeward as the liners
    scurry by.

Thrashing through a tearing gale with a dark green
    sea ahead,
While the funnel-clews sing madly against a sky of
    red,
Foam-choked and wave-choked, scarred by bat-
    tered gear,
The long, brown decks are whirling seas where
    silver combers rear.

Swinging down a brilliant gulf with shores of brown
    and gray,
The snub-nosed, well-decked tankers slowly steam
    their way,

Up the Straits to the Pirate Coast and dim harbor
    of the South
Where they lie like long red patches by a jungle
    river's mouth.

         Gordon Malherbe Hillman

HIGH TIDE AT 4 A.M.

They've tipped and they've shovelled, they've
    trimmed and they've stored,
  And she's down to her load-line as ever;
The bridge is swung round and the pilot's aboard
  And she's off to the dark o' the river.

Farewell to the grime and the dust of the tips,
  It may be a month or for ever:
She's watched by the skeleton ghosts on the slips
  As she ploughs through the dark o' the river.

She is one with the Mill and the Mine and the
    Mart;
  Black coal is her cargo as ever:
You may sneer as you will, but she carries my
    heart
  Way down in the dark o' the river.

So I pray to the Lord in my bed here ashore
  A fair-weather passage to give her,
For there's shipmates aboard I may never see
    more
  Till we've passed through the Dark o' the River!

         William McFee (1909)

THE WATER-FRONT

There are some outlandish brigs and some queer
      foreign rigs,
And schooners and barkentines trim;
Strange craft from Callao and tramps from Bilbao,
White yachts and grey men-o'-war grim.

And a forest of spars soaring up to the stars,
  In ships come from over the sea;
And a smell in the air seems to tempt you to dare
  Ship off—far away—and be free!

Then you question the worth of your counting-
      house berth,
The blood seems to leap in your veins;
And you dream of new places and customs and
      faces
And chafe in despair at your chains.

You go back to your stool and you think what a
      fool
  Is he who's contented to slave
Over profits and losses of hard-fisted bosses—
  Heigh-ho! for a life on the wave.

Anonymous

THE LEADSMAN'S SONG

For England, when with favoring gale
Our gallant ship up Channel steered,
And scudding under easy sail,
The high blue western lands appeared,

To heave the lead the seaman sprang,
And to the pilot cheerly sang:
    "By the deep — Nine."

And bearing up to gain the port,
Some well-known object kept in view,
An abbey tower, a ruined fort,
A beacon to the vessel true;
While oft the lead the seaman flung,
And to the pilot cheerly sung:
    "By the mark — Seven."

And as the much-loved shore we near,
With transport we behold the roof
Where dwelt a friend or partner dear,
Of faith and love and matchless proof.
The lead once more the seaman flung,
And to the watchful pilot sung:
    "Quarter less — Five."

Now to her berth the ship draws nigh,
With slackened sail she feels the tide,
"Stand clear, the cable," is the cry,
The anchor's gone, we safely ride.
The watch is set and through the night,
We hear the seaman with delight
    Proclaim — "All's well."

W. Pearce

THE LUBBER

I've never been a sailor, and I've never been to sea—
It's queer how certain things I love, should bring
    such dreams to me!

The creaking o' a hawser; the marking o' the tide;
And a ship like an eagle with her wings flung
    wide.
    The lean masts — the tall masts;
    The smell o' ropes and tar;
    The thought o' bells to sound the hours;
    The steering by a star.

I never see a ship come in, weary of wind and
    foam —
But I would be aboard her decks, and laughing to
    be home.
I never watch a ship set sail for some far, foreign
    place —
But I'd be in her bows to feel the wind against my
    face.

Folks think that I'm a plodding man, and wedded to
    my ways —
They'd call me daft to know the way I spend my
    holidays:
A-hanging 'round the jetties and the wharves below
    the town,
A-watching and a-wondering 'til the sun goes down.

The rattle o' the winches; the lifting o' the chain;
The singing o' the sailor-men that face the sea
    again.
    Port light — and starboard light;
    The brave bosun's shout —
    But I'm in the harbor,
    And the tide's going out.

Carol Haynes

FOG

The first thing I remember was the fog against the
     pane,
A shroud for many shadows and an aftermath of
     rain,
The high fog, the low fog along the surf-bound
     bay
Where the tall ships swung to leeward to fight the
     crashing spray!

The gray fog, the black fog with scarlet lights and
     rifts,
Where the ruddy light of Sankaty breaks through
     the blank white drifts,
The mist that sweeps across the moors and hides
     the sullen shore,
That draws a flickering curtain where the brazen
     fog horns roar!

The first thing I remember was the strong surf
     groaning,
And the craft offshore, and the sirens moaning,
And the fog drawn like a blanket, a yellow wall of
     gloom
That hid the shelving rocky beach and dulled the
     breakers' boom.

The high fog, the low fog that hides the sea and
     land,
That spreads in sullen ochre till the ruffled sky is
     spanned,

That brings the salt from seaward, and beyond its
    shifting wall
You hear the roaring chorus where the fog-bound
    sea craft call!

Anonymous

THE BALLAD OF THE "BOLIVAR"

Seven men from all the world back to Docks again,
Rolling down the Ratcliffe Road drunk and raising
    Cain.
Give the girls another drink 'fore we sign away —
We that took the "Bolivar" out across the Bay!

We put out from Sunderland loaded down with
    rails;
    We put back to Sunderland 'cause our cargo
      shifted;
We put out from Sunderland — met the winter
    gales —
    Seven days and seven nights to the Start we
      drifted.

    Racketing her rivets loose, smoke-stack white
      as snow,
    All the coals adrift adeck, half the rails below,
    Leaking like a lobster-pot, steering like a
      dray —
    Out we took the *Bolivar,* out across the Bay!

One by one the Lights came up, winked and let us
    by;
    Mile by mile we waddled on, coal and fo'c'sle
      short;

Met a blow that laid us down, heard a bulkhead
     fly;
  Left The Wolf behind us with a two-foot list to
      port.

    Trailing like a wounded duck, working out her
      soul;
    Clanging like a smithy-shop after every roll;
    Just a funnel and a mast lurching through the
      spray —
    So we threshed the *Bolivar* out across the Bay!

Felt her hog and felt her sag, betted when she'd
     break;
  Wondered every time she raced if she'd stand
      the shock;
Heard the seas like drunken men pounding at her
     strake;
  Hoped the Lord 'ud keep his thumb on the
      plummer-block!

    Banged against the iron decks, bilges choked
      with coal;
    Flayed and frozen foot and hand, sick of heart
      and soul;
    'Last we prayed she'd buck herself into Judg-
      ment Day —
    Hi! we cursed the *Bolivar* knocking round the
      Bay!

O! her nose flung up to sky, groaning to be still —
  Up and down and back we went, never time for
     breath;

Then the money paid at Lloyd's caught her by the
    keel,
  And the stars ran 'round and 'round dancin' at
    our death!

    Aching for an hour's sleep, dozing off between;
    'Heard the rotten rivets draw when she took it
      green;
    Watched the compass chase its tail like a cat at
      play —
    That was on the *Bolivar,* south across the Bay!

Once we saw between the squalls, lyin' head to
    swell —
  Mad with work and weariness, wishin' they was
    we —
Some damned Liner's lights go by like a grand
    hotel;
  'Cheered her from the *Bolivar* swampin' in the
    sea.

    Then a greyback cleared us out, then the skip-
      per laughed;
    "Boys, the wheel has gone to Hell — rig the
      winches aft!
    Yoke the kicking rudder-head — get her under
      way!"
    So we steered her, pully-haul, out across the
    Bay!

    Just a pack o' rotten plates puttied up with tar,
    In we came, an' time enough, 'cross Bilbao
    Bar.

Overloaded, undermanned, meant to founder,
  we
Euchred God Almighty's storm, bluffed the
  Eternal Sea!

Seven men from all the world back to town again,
Rollin' down the Ratcliffe Road drunk and raising
  Cain:
Seven men from out of Hell. Ain't the owners gay,
'Cause we took the "Bolivar" *safe across the Bay?*
                          Rudyard Kipling

SEA MOOD

I shut my eyes, and I can see
  How once we all sat on the hold,
And sang the songs that memory
  Had not permitted to grow old.

We sang in seven different tongues,
  And each tongue had its separate tears,
While some would sigh to clear their lungs,
  Breaking the harmony for our ears.

And when we'd stop, some Swede or Dane
  Would swing into his own folk-song,
Then clear his throat, and tell again
  Why he left home, and just how long.

Or, looking at the sea with eyes
  That saw none of the swells and spray,
The scullery-kid who grew man-size
  Amid us, told about the day

He ran away from home to find
    What greater things the earth contains
Than cities filling throats with grind,
    Slit through with narrow, crooked lanes.

Then as the hours grew late, we'd take
    Our last look at the Milky Way
That sprawled across the sky, to break
    The blue, to something one could pray, —

So great it seemed, and we would gaze
    At length upon that holy sight,
Then go below in separate ways
    To clinch the silence of the night.

Milton Raison

THE ANCHOR

By furious fire begotten,
    From patient iron I rose;
Stern hammers were the midwives,
    My birth-caresses, blows.

Of fire that dares and iron that bides
    Thy fierce, grim soul had stuff and form
That flouts the touch and kiss of tides,
    And sets its strength against the storm.

The work to me appointed:
    In coral, mud or sand,
To strike, and grip my hardest —
    And having gripped, to stand.

Unseen thou striv'st, save by dark bulks
  That watch thee struggling in the ooze,
Or staring ports of crusted hulks,
  Or orbless eye-pits of their crews.

The beds of many waters
  Have felt my earnest grip,
That saves from death or straying
  My pretty, foolish ship.

The desperate bark, with strife fordone,
  Sea, earth and air her foemen, trusts
Thy grasp, fell-set where many a one
  Of thy abandoned brethren rusts.

Tho' last they slip my cable
  To save my ship — forlorn,
Forgot, to rust — what matter?
  I shall have striv'n and borne.

Lord God of Effort, grant me such
  A grave as this. Be it my lot
Having done and borne, to sleep, nor much
  To care how much men say, or what.
                                      William Laird

"THE SEA IS A HARP"

There is no music that man has heard
  Like the voice of the minstrel Sea,
Whose major and minor chords are fraught
  With infinite mystery —

There is no passion that man has sung,
  Like the love of the deep-souled Sea,
Whose tide responds to the Moon's soft light
  With marvelous melody —

There is no sorrow that man has known,
  Like the grief of the wordless Main,
Whose Titan bosom forever throbs
  With an untranslated pain —

For the Sea is a harp, and the winds of God
  Play over his rhythmic breast,
And bear on the sweep of their mighty wings
  The song of a vast unrest.

William Hamilton Hayne

OF MARINERS

Sea folk have speech that is not quite their own,
  Twilight is in their talk and sound of water,
For every sea-wife, every sea-wife's daughter
  Knows ships and spars and masts and the sea's
    moan.

Sea folk have speech that is not quite their own,
  For wind is on them and the salty sun,
For every seaman, every seaman's son
  Knows sound of fretting water over stone.

Never a wind that comes from the East again,
  But they must speak of it to mate or friend,
Never a ship comes home in windy rain
  But they must tell it over without end.

Their salty speech is not their own at all,
But sound of water falling by a wall.

Harold Vinal

"SHIPPING NEWS"

Here is the record of their splendid days:
  The curving prow, the tall and stately mast,
And all the width and wonder of their ways
  Reduced to little printed words, at last:
The *Helen Dover* docks, the *Mary Ann*
  Departs for Ceylon and the Eastern trade:
Arrived: *The Jacque,* with cargoes from Japan,
  And *Richard Kidd,* a tramp, — and *Silver Maid.*

The narrow print is wide enough for these:
  But here: "Reported Missing" . . . the type fails,
The column breaks for white, disastrous seas,
  The jagged spars thrust through, and flapping
    sails
Flagging farewells to sky and wind and shore,
  Arrive at silent ports, and leave no more.

David Morton

HERVÉ RIEL
(*May* 31, 1692)

On the sea and at the Hogue, sixteen hundred
    ninety-two,
  Did the English fight the French, — woe to
    France!
And, the thirty-first of May, helter-skelter through
    the blue,

Like a crowd of frightened porpoises a shoal of
  sharks pursue,
  Came crowding ship on ship to Saint Malo on the
  Rance,
With the English fleet in view.

'Twas the squadron that escaped, with the victor in
  full chase;
  First and foremost of the drove, in his great ship,
  Damfreville;
  Close on him fled, great and small,
  Twenty-two good ships in all;
And they signalled to the place:
"Help the winners of a race!
  Get us guidance, give us harbor, take us quick —
  or, quicker still,
  Here's the English can and will!"

Then the pilots of the place put out brisk and leapt
  on board;
  "Why, what hope or chance have ships like these
  to pass?" laughed they:
" Rocks to starboard, rocks to port, all the passage
  scarred and scored,
  Shall the *Formidable* here, with her twelve-and-
  eighty guns
  Think to make the river-mouth by the single
  narrow way, —
Trust to enter where 'tis ticklish for a craft of
  twenty tons,
  And with flow at full beside?
  Now, 'tis slackest ebb of tide.
  Reach the mooring? Rather say,

While rock stands, or water runs,
   Not a ship will leave the bay!"

Then was called a council straight.
Brief and bitter the debate:
"Here's the English at our heels; would you have
      them take in tow
All that's left us of the fleet, linked together stern
      and bow,
For a prize to Plymouth Sound?
Better run the ships aground!"
   (Ended Damfreville his speech).
"Not a minute more to wait!
   Let the Captains, all and each,
   Shove ashore, then blow up, burn the vessels on
      the beach!
France must undergo her fate.

"Give the word!" But no such word
Was ever spoke or heard;
   For up stood, for out stepped, for in struck amid
      all these
— A Captain?   A Lieutenant?   A Mate — first,
      second, third?
   No such man of mark, and meet
   With his betters to compete!
   But a simple Breton sailor pressed by Tourville
      for the fleet,
A poor coasting-pilot he, Hervé Riel the Croi-
      sickese.

And "What mockery or malice have we here?"
      cries Hervé Riel:
   "Are you mad, you Malouins? Are you cowards,
      fools, or rogues?

Talk to me of rocks and shoals, me who took the
    soundings, tell
On my fingers every bank, every shallow, every
    swell
  'Twixt the offing here and Grève where the river
    disembogues?
Are you bought by English gold? Is it love the
    lying's for?
  Morn and eve, night and day,
  Have I piloted your bay,
Entered free and anchored fast at the foot of
    Solidor.
  Burn the fleet and ruin France? That were worse
    than fifty Hogues!
  Sirs, they know I speak the truth! Sirs, believe
    me there's a way!
Only let me lead the line,
  Have the biggest ship to steer,
  Get this *Formidable* clear,
Make the others follow mine,
And I lead them, most and least, by a passage I
    know well,
  Right to Solidor past Grève,
    And there lay them safe and sound;
  And if one ship misbehave,
    — Keel so much as grate the ground,
Why, I've nothing but my life, — here's my head!"
    cries Hervé Riel.

Not a minute more to wait.
"Steer us in, then, small and great!
  Take the helm, lead the line, save the squad-
    ron!" cried its chief.

Captains, give the sailor place!
　He is Admiral, in brief.
Still the north-wind, by God's grace!
See the noble fellow's face
As the big ship, with a bound,
Clears the entry like a hound,
Keeps the passage as its inch of way were the wide
　　　sea's profound!
　　See, safe through shoal and rock,
　　How they follow in a flock,
Not a ship that misbehaves, not a keel that grates
　　　the ground,
　　Not a spar that comes to grief!
The peril, see, is past.
All are harbored to the last,
And just as Hervé Riel holloas "Anchor!" sure as
　　　fate,
Up the English come, too late!

　　So, the storm subsides to calm:
　　They see the green trees wave
　　On the heights o'erlooking Grève.
Hearts that bled are stanched with balm.
　　　"Just our rapture to enhance;
　　　Let the English rake the bay,
　　Gnash their teeth and glare askance
　　　As they cannonade away!
'Neath rampired Solidor pleasant riding on the
　　　Rance!"
How hope succeeds despair on each Captain's
　　　countenance!
Out burst all with one accord,
　　"This is Paradise for Hell!

        Let France, let France's King
        Thank the man that did the thing!"
What a shout, and all one word,
        "Hervé Riel!"
As he stepped in front once more,
        Not a symptom of surprise
        In the frank, blue Breton eyes,
Just the same man as before.

Then said Damfreville, "My friend,
I must speak out at the end,
        Though I find the speaking hard.
Praise is deeper than the lips:
You have saved the King his ships,
        You must name your own reward.
'Faith, our sun was near eclipse!
Demand whate'er you will,
France remains your debtor still.
Ask to heart's content and have! or my name's not
                Damfreville."

Then a beam of fun outbroke
On the bearded mouth that spoke,
As the honest heart laughed through
Those frank eyes of Breton blue:
"Since I needs must say my say,
Since on board the duty's done,
And from Malo Roads to Croisic Point, what is it
        but a run? —
Since 'tis ask and have, I may —
        Since the others go ashore —
Come! A good whole holiday!

Leave to go and see my wife, whom I call the
    Belle Aurore!"
That he asked and that he got, — nothing more.

Name and deed alike are lost:
Not a pillar or a post
    In his Croisic keeps alive the feat as it befell;
Not a head in white and black
On a single fishing-smack,
In memory of the man but for whom had gone to
        wrack
    All that France saved from the fight whence
        England bore the bell.
Go to Paris: rank on rank
    Search the heroes flung pell-mell
On the Louvre, face and flank!
    You shall look long enough ere you come to
        Hervé Riel.
So, for better and for worse,
Hervé Riel, accept my verse!
In my verse, Hervé Riel, do thou once more
Save the squadron, honor France, love thy wife the
    Belle Aurore!

                Robert Browning

"TRAMP STEAMER STANDING OUT, SIR!"

    Tramp, tramp, tramp!
  With a clash and a crash they rise and fall,
  The shining steel beams of the engines tall;
  Whirling the cranks that turn the screw
  That speed our old freight drogher over the
      blue.

Tramp, tramp, tramp!
The din of machinery's music to me,
As we stand down the bay toward the open sea.
Bound for the ports below the line —
"Here, with that oil! Hear that bearing whine?"

Tramp, tramp, tramp!
With boiler tubes clean we are on our way,
And a full head of steam we will have today.
The skipper can worry about the rocks;
I want to know why that engine knocks!

Tramp, tramp, tramp!
Starboard and port with a steady tread,
Never off watch whilst there's work ahead.
Our engines are giants with muscles of steel,
And water and coal is their simple meal.

Tramp, tramp, tramp!
Up to the deck I'll go for a blow;
The shore-line is fading, sure, but slow;
What's that off our beam? A big battle-ship!
Inbound, I guess, from a southern trip.

Tramp, tramp, tramp!
They look mighty slick with their brasswork
bright —
And gosh! They look clean in this sunny light!
There they go, yelling and waving their hats!
What's that they're shouting, the sassy young
brats?
"Tramp, Tramp, Tramp!"

James V. Murray

FISH-WHARF RHAPSODY

To Hell with shop and factory!
To Hell with all stale, musty things —
'Cept musty ale!
The sea for me! The sea!
Where the wind flings the salt spume in your face
And sings and screeches like a sailor on a spree.
We're free, we're going to sea
To fish for flounder and for cod —
Henry and me.
And for thoughts, too and dreams, please God;
And for transcriptions of the free songs of the
        winds:
The elemental chantery, the depths,
The medicinal salt that stings and makes the bleary
        eye,
But brings a clearer vision,
So a man can see that all the fuss and rotten
        trumpery
Of getting and success
Is not for kings —
Kings like Henry and me, — Vikings!
So to Hell with shop and factory!
To Hell with smug respectability!
We're going to sea, Henry and me —
To be free — to be free!

Frederick Manley

BALLAD OF NEW BEDFORD

This be the cry through the long, long night
That darkened the day of a fleet of sail

Whose pulse beat high in the running flight
  On the quest of an oily grail;
Whose logs inked down the Arctic gale
  And the tropic calm as an equal note;
Whose creed rang out in the Spartan hail:
  "A dead whale or a stove boat!"

Morals of scarlet and morals white
  Were mixed in the labor of tooth and nail,
Battle and murder and certain fight
  Of the Kingdom of the Whale;
  Yet in from a far, forgotten, pale,
    Old misty dawn the echoes float
  Of the crystal code of a sea-bred male:
    "A dead whale or a stove boat!"

The pioneer heart of a race whose might
  Was cupped by the bounds of an oaken rail,
Whose eyes dimmed up to the meager sight
  Of a lonely beach of shale,
  Whose mouths grew hard and whose speech
      grew stale,
    And whose pity stuck in the throat,
  Was weighed by a phrase in the Judgment scale:
    "A dead whale or a stove boat!"

Sleepers, down where the sun-beams fail
  To fathom the color of gold or groat —
Chant us again your Godling tale:
  "A dead whale or a stove boat!"

                              Aaron Davis

THE WORLD OF SHIPS

I want to go back to the world of ships;
To the kicking seas where the salt sleet whips;
Where the flying spray will cling and freeze,
And a ten-inch stick will snap in the breeze;
Where a dog's a dog, and a man's a Jack,
Or a man's a cur if his deeds are black.
Just send me back to the world of ships,
   Where a skipper knows his men.

I shipped for a cabin boy at ten,
My lot was cast with hairy men;
Grizzled and rough, but true as steel,
Wicked as Sin, but they were real,
The God they knew was the God of the sea,
And a creed like their's will do for me.
So send me back to the world of ships,
   For I'll know my billet then.

Send me aloft at brail and clew,
Lash me there 'tween blue and blue;
Send me below where the Black-gang heaves,
Where the pistons spit, and the crank-shaft grieves;
Send me on deck with bucket and swab;
Name the packet, and pick my job.
But send me back to the world of ships —
   And I'll be happy again.

        Burt Franklin Jenness

DRAKE'S DRUM

Drake he's in his hammock an' a thousand mile
  away
  (Capten, art tha sleepin' there below?)
Slung atween the round shot in Nombre Dios Bay,
  An' dreamin' arl the time o' Plymouth Hoe.
Yarnder lumes the island, yarnder lie the ships,
  Wi' sailor lads a-dancin' heel-an'-toe,
An' the shore-lights flashin', an' the night-tide
    dashin',
  He sees et arl so plainly as he saw et long ago.

Drake he was a Devon man, an' ruled the Devon
    seas,
  (Capten, art tha sleepin' there below?)
Rovin' tho' his death fell, he went wi' heart at
    ease,
  An' dreamin' arl the time o' Plymouth Hoe.
"Take my drum to England, hang et by the shore,
  Strike et when your powder's runnin' low;
If the Dons sight Devon, I'll quit the port o' Heaven,
  An' drum them up the Channel as we drummed
    them long ago."

Drake he's in his hammock till the great Armadas
    come,
  (Capten, art tha sleepin' there below?),
Slung atween the round shot, listenin' for the
    drum,
  An' dreamin' arl the time o' Plymouth Hoe.
Call him on the deep sea, call him up the Sound,
  Call him when ye sail to meet the foe;

Where the old Trade's plyin' an' the old flag flyin'
    They shall find him ware an' wakin', as they
      found him long ago!
                    Sir Henry Newbolt

THE BOATSWAIN'S STORY

On the first voyage that I ever made,
I had heard so much about the cruel sea
That I expected, when we passed the bar,
Neptune would be howling and throwing water on us.
Instead of that, we had fair weather, weeks and
      weeks,
And a beautiful, dreamy sea
So that I was near afraid to watch the ship break
      through it,
For it was just like tearing silk.
And I thought that then I loved the sea
More than anything I had ever known.

We went to Chow and took for freight
Five hundred immigrants for Madagascar.
All through the China and South China sea
We had such weather that I thought
That it could never storm again; and that life at sea
Must have been rougher in my father's time.
We came into the Indian ocean,
And it was like a lake of glass
With white clouds reflected in it.
The weather was warm, with no breeze.
And we had awnings over the whole ship.
Out on the fore-deck, where the Chinese were,
We had two galleys and a hog-pen on the deck.

One day, when I was on the main deck
Watching those Chinese under the awnings,
The mate came by, saying to the bos'n that the sky
    looked bad.
It did look queer, all right.
And I thought that maybe we would have some
    rain.
While I still was standing there,
Watching two of the Chinese play a game, —
"LOOK OUT! LOOK OUT! LOOK OUT! MY
    GOD! —"
The wind struck us
And the awnings blew away, all at once, —
As a man's clothes are torn off in an explosion.

Then the whole sea lifted, higher than the ship,
And came at us over the fo'cs'le head.
At first I thought that it was all a dream,
Until I saw those Chinamen, and our deck lumber,
And hogs, and big iron kettles from the galley
Pile up against the bridge.
It looked like badly-made Chop Suey.

Some of the Chinamen had broke their arms and
    legs;
And some were all cut up.
The fo'cs'le and all the rooms were wet.
And some got fever from it.
When morning came, we dropped ten overboard,
Not knowing when we would be there ourselves.
After two days, the wind went down.
And bye and bye, the sea was like a lake of glass,
With white clouds in it.

You might have thought old Neptune
Had forgotten how to storm.
But I remembered what was said about the
　　　　cruel sea.
And I understood.

A. Binns

EUTHANASIA

" The Iowa was used as a target and sunk."

Lead sky where planes like vultures soar,
Slate sea where sea-hounds by the score
Swarm in to learn the lesson hoar,
　　How a brave ship may die.

Blind, toothless, clad in mangy rust,
A feeble war-dog, once the Nation's trust,
There to be slain as old dogs must,
　　Their fighting days gone by.

Unmanned, unarmed, she steams for home,
Never again to push the foam,
Never again the seas to roam,
　　With head held proudly high.

Far in the offing, clouds of blue
Belch forth with flames of orange hue,
A gallant ship to give her due,
　　As aged warriors die.

Silence — and then the crash and shock,
As deadly shells her old frame rock,
She gamely turns her foes to mock,
　　Still there when smoke blows by.

In her old sides great, gaping wounds
Let in the sea with strangling sounds:
Her decks aheap with splintered mounds;
   Pillars of smoke rise high.

As an old swordsman grants defeat,
She bows with dignity complete,
And slowly bends the sea to meet,
   In stateliness to die.

Loud in salute guns peal her knell,
The anthem rises o'er the swell
Marking the spot where patriot fell
   In bravest honor high.

Farewell! The seas uncharted sail,
Your dauntless courage will not fail
The search for Freedom's Holy Grail,
   Your spirit never die.

              Colby Rucker

WITH THE SUBMARINES

Above, the baffled twilight fails; beneath, the blind
    snakes creep;
Beside us glides the charnel shark, our pilot
    through the deep;
And, lurking where low headlands shield from
    cruising scout and spy,
We bide the signal through the gloom that bids us
    slay or die.

All watchful, mute, the crouching guns that guard
    the strait sea lanes —
Watchful and hawk-like, plumed with hate, the
    desperate aeroplanes —
And still as death and swift as fate, above the
    darkling coasts,
The spying Wireless sows the night with troops of
    stealthy ghosts,
While hushed through all her huddled streets the
    tide-walled city waits
The drumming thunders that announce brute
    battle at her gates.

Southward a hundred windy leagues, through
    storms that blind and bar,
Our cheated cruisers search the waves, our Cap-
    tains seek the war;
But here the port of peril is; the foeman's dread-
    noughts ride
Sullen and black against the moon, upon a sullen
    tide.
And only we to launch ourselves against their stark
    advance —
To guide uncertain lightnings through these
    treacherous seas of chance!
· · · · · ·

And now a wheeling searchlight paints a signal on
    the night;
And now the bellowing guns are loud with the wild
    lust of fight.
· · · · · ·

And now, her flanks of steel a-pulse with all the
    power of hell,

Forth from the darkness leaps in pride a hateful
    miracle,
The flagship of their Admiral — and now God help
    and save! —
We challenge Death at Death's own game; we sink
    beneath the wave!

    . . . . . .

Ah, steady now — and one good blow — one
    straight stab through the gloom —
Ah, good! the thrust went home! she founders —
    founders to her doom! —
Full speed ahead! — those damned quick-firing
    guns — but let them bark —
What's that — the dynamos? — they've got us,
    men! — *Christ! in the dark!*

                       Don Marquis

THE INCORRIGIBLE

Of all hard lives, the sailor's is the worst;
Toil — hardship — danger — little else beside;
Forever on the move, like one accurst;
His home — his war-bag, and the sea — his bride.

While the trade-wind croons to the tautened sail,
And the golden moon draws a silver trail
Through the waves that lap at the vessel's rail —
While the rosy east grows paler;
He sands the deck, or he scrapes the rail,
Or he lays aloft with a gummy pail
To tar the rigging, or take in sail,
And to damn the life of a sailor.

But I can't peddle ribbons all day long;
Silk shirts, and perfumes! Bah! They stifle me;
I'm lonesome in this senseless, shuffling throng;
I want fresh air, and freedom, and — the sea!

We'll say you go in steam — that's Hell again;
Part stevedore — part flunky — and the rest
Dumb beast; to drudge your measured shift and
        then
Do "overtime" on cargo — "by request."

You wrestle freight in a fetid hold,
Or you coil down lines in the piercing cold,
While the Northern Lights roll, fold on fold,
And mock you for "fools" and "failures."
When the heat-waves blur in the sultry air
You're over the side, in a bosun's chair,
To scrape and paint, and to curse and swear
At the sea, and its ships, and its sailors.

But I can't stand the shop's unceasing din;
The "chanting wheels of progress" madden me;
I want to feel the wind against my skin —
To breathe the salty fragrance of — the sea!

You turn to gas — that's worse than all the rest!
The stink — cramped quarters — grub that drives
        you mad!
A decent berth at sea's a hopeless quest;
There just ain't no such critter to be had.

You hit the banks with fishing-fleet
Where the wind blows the sea-boots off your feet,

And you battle with fog, and snow, and sleet
That would shake the heart of a whaler.
Or you follow the wily salmon's trails
Till your very soul seems caked with scales,
And you swear by all that swims or sails
You will ship no more as a sailor.

But I can't ride a pitchfork all my life;
The clover's fragrance don't appeal to me;
I want the scent of tar — the sense of strife;
Who wouldn't sell a farm and go to sea?

The poet sings of the starry night, and the low-
    swung southern moon;
But the sailor battles with Neptune's might, and the
    wrath of the mad typhoon.
The Southern Cross is a total loss to a soul by hard-
    ship calloused,
And a wave-swept deck breeds scant respect for the
    "Rory Bory Alice."
It's tough to be on the boundless sea, with fire
    'neath your battened hatches;
For there's little chance to court Romance while
    your skin peels off in patches.
You've small desire to invite your soul, or to drink
    in Nature's beauty,
Whilst you breathe the reek from a slimy hold, or
    pursue the lightsome cootie.
It's a hard, and a grim, and a thankless life; no
    profits, and little mirth;
It's a tough old game, but I'd swap that same for no
    other life on earth!

Larry O'Conner

ABANDONED IN THE ICE

There's a blotch to-night on the snow-fields white,
And the frost-locked floe-bergs fret
'Gainst the open sides where a whale-ship rides
With her frozen canvas set.
The star-frost sifts where she dreams and drifts
In the grip of a crystal sea —
But the buried trails of the bowhead whales
Urge her on through eternity.

There's a scented breeze on the southern seas
Where her sister ships decay.
But she laughs at time in that frozen clime
Where the blinding blizzards play.
The auroras flare in the bitter air
Where the deadly ice-dust swirls —
Waking the fires of lost desires
In her cordage of crusted pearls.

Chart Pitt

SAILING ORDERS

If you're weary of the office
    And your step has lost its snap,
If you're looking for a life that fits
    A big, two-fisted chap —
If you want to go a-roving
    All this jolly old world 'round
Come a-running, running, buddy,
    When the bugle starts to sound.

For we've got our sailing orders,
    And there's joy in all our hearts —

Oh, we're dropping down the river
  And it's hey! for foreign parts;
It's hey! for Guam and Haiti
  And the beach at Wai-ki-ki —
The marines have got their orders
  And they're putting out to sea.

They're cheering from the ferries,
  And they're waving from the shore;
The dull old life's behind us
  And the new life lies before;
We're off to make talk "howdy"
  With the Moro and Chinee —
The marines have got their orders
  And they're putting out to sea.

Anonymous

RUNNING THE EASTING DOWN

From Cape Good Hope to Melbourne, with yards
  squared taut and true,
We drove East under fore course and a rag of
  tops'ls too.
The following seas ran close astern, deep troughed
  and crested white —
Sea horses fearful in the day, mad chargers in the
  night.
With head in spray, 'mid spuming drift, beneath a
  leaden sky,
We held our course 'fore the westerly gales as the
  Southern sea birds fly.
In sixty east and forty south, as near as we could
  say,

We shipped a sea in the last dog-watch that washed
the wheel away.
To starboard went the helmsman, lashed to the
broken rim,
The mad blue water swept the deck and two men
followed him.
"Aft to the rudder-tackles!" God! How she
thrashed about —
"Man the lee fore braces!" we heard the Captain
shout.
Next she took a comber high on the quarter rail,
As ready hands 'way forward braced sharp the
great foresail.
The weather leeches stiffened, she ran up, then fell
off,
And a cable payed from the quarter-bitts steadied
her 'cross the trough.
But aft in the black sea boiling lay death 'neath the
storm clouds' frown,
In sixty east and forty south when running the
Easting down.

Felix Riesenberg

ISLANDS

There is something about islands which no printed
words convey;
They are magnets; why, we cannot quite explain.
Is it that a ring of water grants our wish to break
away
From the iron grooves we poke along for gain?
There's magic (that is certain), lasting magic (that
is sure)

About islands which affects both young and gray;
And treasure-trove of pirate gold can hardly be the
      lure,
For their magic is as old as night and day.

Siren old, it called to nations when Phœnecia rode
      the sea
And when ancient Greece and Rome went South
      and West;
To Saxon, Viking, Englishman, to Don and Portu-
      gee,
While minstrels sang the Islands of the Blest.
There's magic (you have felt it), haunting magic
      (how it grips)
About islands (hillman, plainsman, though you
      be)
Which stirs you as a boy is stirred by driving full-
      rigged ships;
It's as natural as the instinct to be free!

                 Richard Butler Glaenzer

THE TOPS'L SCHOONER

(*The Pirate Craft Speaks*)

You fear no more to see my sails
    Come sweeping up the seas,
Nor guard with pike and carronade
    Your laden argosies;
You never turn and run for it
    When the lookout bellows now:
"There's a low, black, tops'l schooner
    Just off the starboard bow!"

You trudge the sea in sordidness,
  And find a sordid grave;
Collision, ice, or hurricane —
  You'll die a burdened slave,
And never know the ecstasy
  Of a hot fight, hand to hand,
With a low, black, tops'l schooner,
  An hundred leagues from land!

You'll never smell the powder,
  Nor feel your hair-roots rouse
When the "long nine" sends its warning
  Across your questing bows;
When the round shot splits the foremast
  And your sturdy spirits fail
As the low, black tops'l schooner
  Pours men across your rail.

No more you'll make the Indies
  With clumsy "ninety-fours,"
And strand on hidden coral-reefs
  Off fever-ridden shores;
I showed your nimblest frigates
  The cleanest pair of heels —
The low, black tops'l schooner,
  That never dawn reveals.

For now my snuggest harbor
  Shall see me ne'er again,
And now my safest anchorage
  Shall wait for me in vain;
A ghost-ship manned by phantoms,
  From Morgan down to Kidd,

The tops'l schooner's left for aye
The islands where she hid.

You fear no more to see my sails
Come sweeping up the seas,
Nor guard with pike and carronade
Your laden argosies;
You never turn and run for it
When the lookout bellows now:
"There's a low, black tops'l schooner
Just off the starboard bow!"

Kenneth Rand

A PAGAN HYMN

I have drunk the Sea's good wine,
And to-day
Care has bowed his head and gone away.
I have drunk the Sea's good wine,
Was ever step so light as mine,
Was ever heart so gay?
Old voices intermingle in my brain,
Voices that a little boy might hear,
And dreams like fiery sunsets come again,
Informulate and vain,
But great with glories of the buccaneer.
Oh, thanks to thee, great Mother, thanks to thee,
For this old joy renewed,
For tightened sinew and clear blood imbued
With sunlight and with sea.
Behold, I sing a pagan song of old,
And out of my full heart,
Hold forth my hands that so I would enfold
The Infinite thou art.

What matter all the creeds that come and go,
The many gods of men?
My blood outcasts them from its joyous flow,
And it is now as then —
The Pearl of Morning, and the Sapphire Sea,
The Diamond of Noon,
The Ruby of the Sunset — these shall be
My creed, my Deity;
And I will take some old forgotten tune,
And rhythm frolic-free,
And sing in little words thy wondrous boon,
O Sunlight and O Sea!

                                        John Runcie

FREIGHTERS

Whenever I wake in the morning
    And the smell of the sea is strong,
My heart becomes filled with yearning
    As my soul becomes filled with song,
And it's all I can do to prevent me
    Going down to the docks right away
And boarding the very first freighter,
The very first salt-spattered freighter,
That's sailing for ports far to eastward
    And is heading for down-the-bay.

Now, passenger ships are like ladies,
    And timid they be with fears;
They know not the wander-spirit
    As they lie at their painted piers,
And like ladies they stick to the fair ways
    Where never a buccaneer trod, —
But any old salt-spattered freighter,

Oh, any old time-honored freighter,
Will sail to the uncharted islands
   And steer by its trust in God.

So whenever I wake in the morning
   And the lure of the sea is there,
It's adventure that calls me, calls me,
   And never was call so fair,
And it's all I can do to prevent me
   Going down to the docks right away
And boarding the very first freighter,
The very first dream-laden freighter,
That's headed for fathomless oceans
   Down the path of the dawning day!
                    Edmund Leamy

THE FIRST AMERICAN SAILORS

Five fearless knights of the first renown
  In Elizabeth's great array,
From Plymouth in Devon sailed up and down —
  American sailors they
    Who went to the West,
    For they all knew best
      Where the silver was gray
      As a moonlit night,
      And the gold as bright
    As a midsummer day —
    A-sailing away
  Through the salt sea spray,
    The first American sailors.

SIR HUMPHREY GILBERT, he was ONE
  And Devon was heaven to him,

He loved the seas as he loved the sun
And hated the Don as the Devil's limb—
Hated him up to the brim!
In Holland the Spanish hide he tanned,
He roughed and routed their braggart band,
And God was with him on sea and land;
Newfoundland knew him, and all that coast,
For he was one of America's host—
And now there is nothing but English speech
For leagues and leagues, and reach on reach,
From near the Equator away to the Pole;
While the billows beat and the oceans roll
On the Three Americas.

SIR FRANCIS DRAKE, and he was TWO
And Devon was heaven to him,
He loved in his heart the waters blue
And hated the Don as the Devil's limb—
Hated him up to the brim!
At Cadiz he singed the King's black beard,
The Armada met him and fled afeard,
Great Philip's golden fleece he sheared;
Oregon knew him, and all that coast,
For he was one of America's host—
And now there is nothing but English speech
For leagues and leagues, and reach on reach,
From California away to the Pole;
While the billows beat and the oceans roll
On the Three Americas.

SIR WALTER RALEIGH, he was THREE
And Devon was heaven to him,

There was nothing he loved so well as the sea ·—
  He hated the Don as the Devil's limb —
    Hated him up to the brim!
He settled full many a Spanish score,
Full many's the banner his bullets tore
On English, American, Spanish shore;
  Guiana knew him, and all that coast,
  For he was one of America's host —
And now there is nothing but English speech
For leagues and leagues, and reach on reach
  From Guiana northward to the Pole;
  While the billows beat and the oceans roll
    On the Three Americas.

SIR RICHARD GRENVILLE, he was FOUR
  And Devon was heaven to him,
He loved the waves and their windy roar
  And hated the Don as the Devil's limb —
    Hated him up to the brim!
He whipped him on land and mocked him at sea,
He laughed to scorn his sovereignty,
And with the *Revenge* beat his "fifty-three";
  Virginia knew him, and all that coast,
  For he was one of America's host —
And now there is nothing but English speech
For leagues and leagues, and reach on reach,
  From the Old Dominion away to the Pole;
  While the billows beat and the oceans roll
    On the Three Americas.

And SIR JOHN HAWKINS, he was FIVE
  And Devon was heaven to him,

He worshipped the water while he was alive
And hated the Don as the Devil's limb —
Hated him up to the brim!
He chased him over the Spanish Main,
His cities he ravished again and again,
He scoffed and defied the navies of Spain;
　The Gulf it knew him, and all that coast,
　For he was one of America's host —
And now there is nothing but English speech
For leagues and leagues, and reach on reach,
　From the Rio Grande away to the Pole;
　While the billows beat and the oceans roll
　　On the Three Americas.

Five fearless knights have filled gallant graves
　This many and many a day,
Some under the willows, some under the waves —
　American sailors they;
　　And still in the West
　　Is their valor blest,
　　　Where a banner bright
　　　　With the ocean's blue
　　　　And the red wrack's hue
　　　And the spoondrift's white
　　　Is smiling to-day
　Through the salt sea spray
　Upon American sailors.

Wallace Rice

TO A SAILOR BURIED ASHORE

He who but yesterday would roam
　Careless as clouds and currents range,

In homeless wandering most at home,
  Inhabiter of change;

Who wooed the West to win the East,
  And named the stars of North and South,
And felt the zest of Freedom's feast
  Familiar in his mouth;

Who found a faith in stranger speech,
  And fellowship in foreign hands,
And had within his eager reach
  The relish of all lands —

How circumscribed a plot of earth
  Keeps now his restless footsteps still,
Whose wish was wide as ocean's girth,
  Whose will the water's will!
                    Charles G. D. Roberts

THE DERELICT

I left her headed for Lord-knows-where, in lati-
    tude forty-nine,
With a cargo of deals from Puget Sound and her
    bows blown off by a mine;
I saw her just as the sun went down; I saw her —
    floating still,
And "I hope them deals will let her sink afore so
    long," said Bill.

It warn't no use to stand by her; she could
    neither sail nor steer,
With the better part of a thousand miles between
    her and Cape Clear.

The sea was up to her water ways, and gaining
fast below,
But I'd like to know that she went to her rest as a
ship has a right to go.

For it's bitter hard on a decent ship, look at it
how you may,
When she's worked her traverse and done her
trick and sailed with the best in her day,
To be floatin' around like a nine-day drowned on
the Western Ocean swell,
With never a one to hand and reef or steer and
strike the bell:

No one to light 'er binnacle lamps an' see they're
burnin' bright,
Or scour her planking, or scrape her seams when
the days are sunny and bright;
No one to sit on her hatch and smoke and yarn
when the day was done,
And say, "That gear wants reevin' new some fine
dog-watch, my son!"

No one to stand by the halyard pin when it's
comin' on to blow;
Never the roar of "Rio Grande" to the watch's
stamp and go;
Just the sea-birds sittin' along the rail and callin'
the long day through
Like the souls of old dead sailormen that used to
be her crew.

Never a port of all her ports for her to fetch
    again;
Nothing; only the sea and the sky, the sun and the
    wind and the rain.
  It's cruel hard on a decent ship, and so I tell you
    true
That I wish I knew she had gone to her rest as a
    good ship ought to do.

C. Fox Smith

PORTRAIT OF A SAILOR

Humped o'er the rail, eyes on the sea he stands,
A filling figure of a man whose hands
Have never touched an object light enough
To do it reverence; — the sacred stuff
Of love, forbearance, faith, he never knew.
And he is cruel in his sportive way,
And cunning in his mischief-making too;
He has no further use for any day,
But take it as it comes and live it through.
Grumbling at sea, carousing in a port,
And so again — that circle's his retort
To all the beauty molded out for him.
Strange his keen eyes should be so sadly dim!
What is the saving grace that made him loved,
Written about and praised where'er he roved?
Truly I do not know, but seeing there,
His figure by the rail, his eyes to sea,
His red face crinkled, and the wind in his hair —
I do not dare deny his majesty.

Milton Raison

THE SQUARE PEG

From my office-cell I saw you towing slowly down
    the sound
With your dirty bilges burdened with a cargo out-
    ward bound.
And I mark the day you claimed me, when I
    sweated in your waist,
When I munched your wormy biscuit with a curse
    between each taste.
Too, I mark the kicks and cuffings at the Dutch-
    man's horny hands
While the booming seas we battled off the shores
    of distant lands.
So I cursed you and reviled you — you and all your
    brutal ken,
And I'd given every dollar to be free of you again.

Now I'm educated — risen — and my hands are
    soft and white;
In the days I drive at figures, but when comes the
    city's night,
Then I see the blowy reaches of the tireless, tossing
    sea.
And I feel the West wind calling as it used to call to
    me;
In my dreams I hear the block-songs, and I skip on
    skys'l yard
With the vivid thrill of knowing that grim death
    may play his card.
Yes, I cursed you, and reviled you, but my thoughts
    have changed since then,
And I'd give my bottom dollar just to tread your
    decks again.

For I'm tired of men and cities, and I think they're
    tired of me;
And my eyes cry out for surcease from the people
    that they see —
Men with pallid, servile manners, men with small
    ambitions vain,
And the ceaseless tide of women with their faces
    marked with pain.
And I feel my fingers itching for the bite of icy
    tacks,
For the rough-and-tumble fighting and the sheets
    that broke men's backs.
You're a rolling, rotten hooker, and your peak's a
    vermin pen,
But I'd give my bottom dollar just to tread your
    decks again.

Gordon Seagrove

SEA SONG

I have lent myself to thy will, O Sea!
    To the urge of thy tidal sway;
My soul to thy lure of mystery,
    My cheek to thy lashing spray.
      For there's never a man whose blood runs
        warm
      But would quaff the wine of the brimming
        storm.
As the prodigal lends have I lent to thee,
    For a day or a year and a day.

And what if the tale be quickly told
    And the voyage be wild and brief?

I can face thy fury with courage bold
  And never a whine of grief,
    Though peril-fanged is thy grisly track,
    The ship goes out that never comes back,
And the sailor's whitened bones are rolled
  In the surge of the whitening reef.

The shores recede, the great sails fill,
  The lee rail hisses under,
As we double the cape of Lighthouse Hill
  Where sea and harbor sunder.
    Then here's to a season of glad unrest!
    With an anchor of hope on the seaman's
    breast,
Till I claim once more from thy savage will
  A soul that is fraught with wonder.

Charles Wharton Stork

SING A SONG OF STEERAGE

Sing a song of steerage, for that's the place to be,
Seven quid will do it, and seven days at sea,
Seven grey December days, keeping near the rail —
And all the little candles are waiting on the tree!

Seven days of porridge, and cabbages and pork,
Seven days of steerage-deck, swinging as you
    walk,
And then the dark blue water is turning yellow-
    brown —
There's the dear old Statue — and it's Christmas
    in New York.

You who cross the channel from Dover to Calais,
You who dress for dinner and go first-class all the
      way,
I wonder will you ever know the thrill that I shall
      feel
When the stately old *Caronia* goes rolling up the
      Bay!

It's a greasy, queasy business a-traveling in the
      third,
Where the meat is mostly horses and the milk is
      chiefly curd,
But it's better to go steerage than not to go at all —
You'll be jolly glad you did it, I give my plighted
      word.

Then sing a song of steerage, for that's the place to
      be,
Seven quid will do it, and seven days at sea;
Seven grey December days, keeping near the
      rail —
And over in America there's Someone waits for me.
                     Christopher Morley
                        (Oxford, 1912)

OF THE LOST SHIP

"What has become of the good ship *Kite?*
  Where is her hull of chosen oak?
Who were the Victors, what the Fight?
The Old Wives — whom did they invoke,
That should tell them so uncannily:

  "Fell through a crack in the Floor of the Sea?"

"Trafficked with death in a cruise foredone,"
The Preachers drone to the Salem Folk,
When the Sea has swallowed up the Sun
And the white gulls glint — was it they who
spoke?
Wes'-Sou'-West from the Devil's Quay:

"Fell through a crack in the Floor of the Sea?"

Though ye searched the West to the guttering sun
Or the East till the baffled lights turn black,
Or North to the bergs till the South be won
The changeling shadows answer back,
And their trembling lips pale piteously:

"Fell through a crack in the Floor of the Sea?"

And when the great grim Finger becks
The whining Seas from their ancient bed,
Shall some tongue speak from the world-old
wrecks
To read the log of the Thwarted Dead?
Is there never an end on the mystery:

"Fell through a crack in the Floor of the Sea?"

Eugene R. White

THE "REVENGE"

(A Ballad of the Fleet, September, 1591)

At Florés in the Azores Sir Richard Grenville lay,
And a pinnace, like a fluttered bird, came flying
from far away:

"Spanish ships of war at sea! We have sighted
    fifty-three!"
Then sware Lord Thomas Howard: "'Fore God I
    am no coward;
But I cannot meet them here, for my ships are out
    of gear,
And the half my men are sick. I must fly, but
    follow quick.
We are six ships of the line; can we fight with
    fifty-three?"

Then spake Sir Richard Grenville: "I know you are
    no coward;
You fly them for a moment to fight with them
    again.
But I've ninety men and more that are lying sick
    ashore.
I should count myself the coward if I left them, my
    Lord Howard,
To these Inquisition dogs and the devildoms of
    Spain."

So Lord Howard passed away with five ships of war
    that day,
Till he melted like a cloud in the silent summer
    heaven;
But Sir Richard bore in hand all his sick men from
    the land
Very carefully and slow,
Men of Bideford in Devon,
And we laid them on the ballast down below;
For we brought them all aboard,

And they blessed him in their pain, that they were
    not left to Spain,
To the thumbscrew and the stake, for the glory of
    the Lord.

He had only a hundred seamen to work the ship
    and to fight,
And he sailed away from Florés till the Spaniard
    came in sight,
With his huge sea-castles heaving upon the
    weather bow.
"Shall we fight or shall we fly?
Good Sir Richard, tell us now,
For to fight is but to die!
There'll be little of us left by the time this sun be
    set."
And Sir Richard said again: "We be all good
    English men.
Let us bang these dogs of Seville, the children of
    the devil,
For I never turned my back upon Don or devil
    yet."

Sir Richard spoke and he laughed, and we roared
    a hurrah, and so
The little *Revenge* ran on sheer into the heart of
    the foe,
With her hundred fighters on deck, and her ninety
    sick below;
For half of their fleet to the right and half to the
    left were seen,
And the little *Revenge* ran on through the long sea-
    lane between.

Thousands of their soldiers looked down from their
    decks and laughed,
Thousands of their seamen made mock at the mad
    little craft
Running on and on, till delayed
By their mountain-like *San Philip* that, of fifteen
    hundred tons,
And up-shadowing high above us with her yawning
    tiers of guns,
Took the breath from our sails, and we stayed.

And while now the great *San Philip* hung above us
    like a cloud
Whence the thunderbolt will fall
Long and loud,
Four galleons drew away
From the Spanish fleet that day,
And two upon the larboard and two upon the star-
    board lay,
And the battle-thunder broke from them all.

But anon the great *San Philip,* she bethought her-
    self and went,
Having that within her womb that had left her ill
    content;
And the rest they came aboard us, and they fought
    us hand to hand,
For a dozen times they came with their pikes and
    musqueteers,
And a dozen times we shook 'em off as a dog that
    shakes his ears
When he leaps from the water to the land.

And the sun went down, and the stars came out far
    over the summer sea,
But never a moment ceased the fight of the one and
    the fifty-three;
Ship after ship, the whole night long, their high-
    built galleons came,
Ship after ship, the whole night long, with her
    battle-thunder and flame;
Ship after ship, the whole night long, drew back
    with her dead and her shame.
For some were sunk and many were shattered, and
    so could fight us no more —
God of battles! Was ever a battle like this in the
    world before?

For he said, "Fight on! fight on!"
Though his vessel was all but a wreck;
And it chanced that when half of the short summer
    night was gone,
With a grisly wound to be dressed he had left the
    deck —
But a bullet struck him that was dressing it sud-
    denly dead,
And himself he was wounded again in the side and
    in the head,
And he said, "Fight on! fight on!"

And the night went down, and the sun smiled out
    far over the summer sea,
And the Spanish fleet with broken sides lay round
    us all in a ring;
But they dared not touch us again, for they feared
    that we still could sting,

So they watched what the end would be.
And we had not fought them in vain,
But in perilous plight were we,
Seeing forty of our poor hundred were slain,
And half of the rest of us maimed for life
In the crash of the cannonades and the desperate
strife;
And the sick men down in the hold were most of
them stark and cold,
And the pikes were all broken or bent, and the
powder was all of it spent;
And the masts and the rigging were lying over the
side;
But Sir Richard cried in his English pride:
"We have fought such a fight for a day and a night
As may never be fought again!
We have won great glory, my men!
And a day less or more
At sea or ashore,
We die — does it matter when?
Sink me the ship, Master Gunner — sink her, split
her in twain!
Fall into the hands of God, not into the hands of
Spain!"

And the gunner said, "Ay, ay," but the seamen
made reply:
"We have children, we have wives,
And the Lord hath spared our lives.
We will make the Spaniard promise, if we yield, to
let us go;
We shall live to fight again and to strike another
blow."

And the lion there lay dying, and they yielded to the
    foe.
And the stately Spanish men to their flagship bore
    him then,
Where they laid him by the mast, old Sir Richard
    caught at last;
And they praised him to his face with their courtly
    foreign grace;
But he rose upon their decks, and he cried:
"I have fought for Queen and Faith like a valiant
    man and true;
I have only done my duty as a man is bound to do.
With a joyful spirit I, Sir Richard Grenville, die!"
And he fell upon their decks, and he died.

And they stared at the dead that had been so
    valiant and true,
And had holden the power and glory of Spain so
    cheap
That he dared her with one little ship and his
    English few;
Was he devil or man? He was devil for aught they
    knew,
But they sank his body with honor down into the
    deep,
And they manned the *Revenge* with a swarthier,
    alien crew,
And away she sailed with her loss and longed for
    her own;
When a wind from the lands they had ruined awoke
    from sleep,
And the water began to heave and the weather to
    moan,

And or ever that evening ended a great gale blew,
And a wave like the wave that is raised by an earth-
quake grew,
Till it smote on their hulls and their sails and their
masts and their flags,
And the whole sea plunged and fell on the shot-
shattered navy of Spain,
And the little *Revenge* herself went down by the
island crags
To be lost evermore in the main.

Alfred Tennyson

SONG FOR ALL SEAS, ALL SHIPS
I

To-day a rude brief recitative,
Of ships sailing the seas, each with its special flag
or ship-signal,
Of unnamed heroes in the ships — of waves
spreading and spreading far as the eye can
reach,
Of dashing spray, and the winds piping and
blowing,
And out of these a chant for the sailors of all
nations,
Fitful, like a surge.

Of sea-captains young or old, and the mates, and
of all intrepid sailors,
Of the few, very choice, taciturn, whom fate can
never surprise nor death dismay,
Picked sparingly without noise by thee, old ocean,
chosen by thee,

Thou sea that pickest and cullest the race in time,
  and unitest nations,
Suckled by thee, old husky nurse, embodying thee,
Indomitable, untamed as thee.

(Ever the heroes on water or on land, by ones or
  twos appearing,
Ever the stock preserved and never lost, though
  rare, enough for seed preserved.)

II

Flaunt out O sea, your separate flags of nations!
Flaunt out visible as ever the various ship-signals!
But do you reserve especially for yourself and for
  the soul of man one flag above all the rest,
A spiritual woven signal for all nations, emblem of
  man elate above death,
Token of all brave captains and all intrepid sailors
  and mates,
And all that went down doing their duty,
Reminiscent of them, twined from all intrepid
  captains young or old,
A pennant universal, subtly waving all time, o'er
  all brave sailors,
All seas, all ships.

Walt Whitman

THE THREE SHIPS

I had tramped along through dockland till the day
  was all but spent,
But for all the ships I there did find I could not be
  content;

By the good pull-ups for car-men and the Chinese
     dives I passed,
And the streets of grimy houses each one grimier
     than the last,
And the shops whose shoddy oilskins many a
     sailorman has cursed
In the wintry Western ocean when it's weather of
     the worst —
All among the noisy graving docks and waterside
     saloons
And the pubs with punk pianos grinding out their
     last year's tunes,
And the rattle of the winches handling freights
     from near and far;
And the whiffs of oil and engines, and the smells of
     bilge and tar;
And of all the craft I came across, the finest for to
     see
Was a dandy ocean liner — but she wasn't meant
     for me!

She was smart as any lady, and the place was fair
     alive
With the swarms of cooks and waiters, just like
     bees about a hive;
It was nigh her time for sailing, and a man could
     hardly stir
For the piles of rich folks' dunnage here and there
     and everywhere.
But the stewards and the awnings and the white
     paint and the gold
Take a deal o' living up to for a chap that's getting
     old;

And the mailboat life's a fine one, but a shellback
        likes to be
Where he feels a kind o' homelike after half his life
        at sea.

    So I sighed and passed her by — "Fare you well,
        my dear," said I,
        "You're as smart and you're as dainty as can be;
    You're a lady through and through, but I know it
        wouldn't do —
    You're a bit too much a rich man's gal for me!"

So I rambled on through dockland, but I couldn't
        seem to find
Out of all the craft I saw there just the one to
        please my mind;
There were tramps and there were tankers, there
        were freighters large and small,
There were concrete ships and standard ships and
        motor ships and all,
And of all the blessed shooting-match the one I
        liked the best
Was a saucy topsail schooner from some harbour in
        the West.

She was neat and she was pretty as a country lass
        should be,
And the girl's name on her counter seemed to suit
        her to a T;
You could almost smell the roses, almost see the
        red and green
Of the Devon plough and pasture where her home
        port must have been,

And I'll swear her blocks were creaking in a kind o'
      Devon drawl —
Oh, she took my fancy rarely, but I left her after
      all!
For it's well enough, is coasting, when the summer
      days are long,
And the summer hours slip by you just as sweetly
      as a song,
When you catch the scent of clover blowing to you
      off the shore,
And there's scarce a ripple breaking from the
      Land's End to the Nore;

But I like a bit more sea-room when the short dark
      days come in,
And the Channel gales and sea-fogs and the nights
      as black as sin,
When you're groping in a fairway that's as crowded
      as a town
With the whole damned Channel traffic looking out
      to run you down,
Or a bloody lee shore's waiting with its fierce and
      foaming lips
For the bones of poor drowned sailormen and
      broken ribs of ships.

  So I sighed and shook my head — "Fare you
      well, my dear," I said,
    "You're a bit too fond o' soundings, lass, for
      me;
  Oh, you're Devon's own dear daughter — but my
      fancy's for deep water
    And I think I'll set a course for open sea!"

So I tramped along through dockland, through the
    Isle of Dogs I went,
But for all the ships I found there still I couldn't be
    content,
Till, not far from Millwall Basin, in a dingy, dreary
    pond,
Mouldy wharf-sheds all around it and a breaker's
    yard beyond,
With its piles of rusty anchors and chain-cables
    large and small,
Broken bones of ships forgotten — there I found
    her after all!
She was foul from West Coast harbours, she was
    worn with wind and tide,
There was paint on all the bright work that was
    once her captain's pride,
And her gear was like a junk-store, and her decks a
    shame to see,
And her shrouds they wanted rattling down as
    badly as could be;

But she lay there on the water just as graceful as a
    gull,
Keeping some old builder's secret in her strong and
    slender hull;
By her splendid sweep of sheer-line and her clean,
    keen clipper bow
You might know she'd been a beauty, and, by God,
    she was one now!
And the river gulls were crying, and the sluggish
    river tide
Made a kind of running whisper by her red and
    rusted side,

And the river breeze came murmuring her tattered
    gear among,
Like some old shellback, known of old, that sings a
    sailor's song,
That whistles through his yellow teeth an old deep-
    water tune
(The same did make the windows shake in the
    Boomerang Saloon!),
Or by the steersman's elbow stays to tell a sea-
    man's tale
About the skippers and the crews in great old days
    of sail!

  And I said: "My dear, although you are growing
    old, I know,
    And as crazy and as cranky as can be,
  If you'll take me for your lover, oh we'll sail the
    wide seas over,
    You're the ship among them all that's meant
    for me!"

                        C. Fox Smith

ON FIRST SEEING THE OCEAN

    And *this* is the dreamed-of wonder!
      This — at last — is the sea!
    Billows of liquid thunder —
      Vocal immensity!
    But where is the thrill of glory
      Born of a great surprise?
    This is the old, old story;
      These are the ancient skies.

Child of the prairie expanses,
   Often the soul of me
Hungered for long sea-glances;
   And here — at last — is the sea.
Yon goes a sea-gull flying;
   There is a sinking mast;
This is the ocean crying!
   This is the rune of the Vast!

But out in my mother country,
   Ever since I was born,
This is the song my brother Winds
   Sang in the fields of corn.
And there, in the purple midnights
   Sullen and still with heat,
This is the selfsame drone that ran
   Over the heading wheat.

Ere Time, the mystical Motion,
   Mothered and cradled thee,
This was the song, O Ocean,
   That saddened the soul of me.
And I long to be as the steamer
   That dwindles, dissolves in the Blue;
For mine is the soul of the dreamer —
   And nothing to me is new.

John G. Neihardt

THE OLD PILOT SPEAKS

Scarce and scarcer grow the ships, wild swans on
      the bay,
Tacking slowly by the marshes of Henlopen and
      Cape May.

The silver ships, the winged ships, like birds have
flown away.
Now it's liners, cargo vessels, wanderin' tramps
come in to port.
Bigger money, but, oh, damn it! give me back the
grand old sport.

As 'prentice lads we roamed the bay with every
breeze that blew
Many's the storm and icy gale that we have weath-
ered through.
A ship ahoy! the pilot sloops would spread their
wings and race
The combers gleaming mountain-high, spray blow-
ing wild like lace.

I've rolled through many a misty night, lightless, till
morning came
To cheat a rival of a ship — our lives staked on the
game.
In the blinding, howling tempest we'd board a
schooner's side,
Our rolling dories pitching like a swiftly bucking
tide.

On outbound ships the mutineers would fight till
decks were red.
"The wilder fight, the better crew," one time the
captain said.

Now the ships come in to find us on a yacht of
newest beam.
Guys in jackets bring ye sodas in a cabin warmed
by steam,

Yet I long for the adventure when the silver ships
     broke free,
Wooing kisses like a sweetheart as they leaped into
     the sea.

Phœbe Hoffman

THE STALKING OF THE SEA-WOLVES

They had come from out of the East
    To ravage and burn and kill,
And they stopped for a moment to rest and wait
    In a landlocked harbor, still.
But a grim sea-dog there was
    Who had stalked them through spray and foam:
And he came, and he looked, and he smiled, and he
     said: —
    "They'll never get home!"

Then another old sea-dog came,
    And they sat them down to wait,
Untiring, stern, through long, dry days,
    At the harbor's frowning gate.
Under the hot, fierce sun,
    Under the still, blue dome,
The sea-dogs waited, and watched, and growled: —
    "They'll never get home!"

And the wolves came forth at last,
    And the grim sea-dogs closed in,
And the battle was won, and the Old Flag waved
    Where the banner of Spain had been.
The colors of blood and gold
    Sank deep in the churning foam,

And the sea-dogs growled: "We have kept our
    word: —
  They'll never get home!"

Cheers for the vow well kept!
  To the sea-dogs twain a toast!
From our land's birth-throes have our sea-dogs
    been
  Our glory, pride, and boast.
Whatever our perils be
  In the unseen years to come,
Our trust is in men like the man who said: —
  "They'll never get home!"

Charles W. Thompson

DEEP-WATER SONG

The bounding deck beneath me,
  The rocking sky o'erhead,
White, flying spume that whips her boom
  And all her canvas spread.

Her topmast rakes the zenith
  Where planets shoal and spawn,
And to her stride God opens wide
  The storm-red gates of dawn.

Then walk her down to Rio,
  Roll her 'cross the line;
Chinee Joe's a-tendin' door
  Down to Number Nine.
Deep they lie in every sea,
  Land's End to the Horn, —

For every sailorman that dies
   A sailorman is born.

Along the battered sea-wall,
   Our women in the rain
Full wearily have scanned the sea
   That brings us not again.

Oh, I'll come home, my dearie;
   Aye, one day I'll come home,
With heaped-up hold of Spanish gold
   And opals of spun foam.

Then walk her down to Frisco,
   Lay her for Hong Kong,
Reeling down the water-front
   Seven hundred strong.
Deep they lie in every sea,
   Land's End to the Horn, —
For every sailorman that dies
   A sailorman is born.

Tall, languid palms that glimmer,
   Blossoms beyond belief,
Sea-gods at play in spouting spray
   On sun-splashed coral reef.

O falling star at twilight!
   O questing sail unfurled!
Through unknown seas I follow these
   Down-hill across the world.

Then walk her down to Sydney,
   Through to Singapore,

Dutch Marie and Ysabel,
  Waitin' on the shore.
Deep they lie in every sea,
  Land's End to the Horn, —
For every sailorman that dies
  A sailorman is born.

                              John Reed

IN LIGHTER VEIN

GREEN ESCAPE

At three o'clock in the afternoon
  On a hot September day,
I began to dream of a highland stream
  And a frostbit russet tree;
Of the swashing dip of a clipper ship
  — White canvas wet with spray —
And the swirling green and milk-foam clean
  Along her canted lee.

I heard the quick staccato click
  Of the typist's pounding keys,
And I had to brood of a wind more rude
  Than that by a motor fanned —
And I lay inert in a flannel shirt
  To watch the rhyming seas
Deploy and fall in a silver sprawl
  On a beach of sun-blanched sand.

There is no desk shall tame my lust
  For hills and windy skies;
My secret hope of the sea's blue slope
  No clerkly task shall dull;
And though I print no echoed hint
  Of adventures I devise,
My eyes still pine for the comely line
  Of an outbound vessel's hull.

When I elope with an autumn day
  And make my green escape,
I'll leave my pen to tamer men
  Who have more docile souls;

For forest aisles and office files
  Have a very different shape,
And it's hard to woo the ocean blue
  In a row of pigeon holes!

Christopher Morley

"DRINK TO THE MEN WHO HAVE GONE ASHORE"

The Skipper and Chief have gone ashore
  And each is a married man,
So I'll tell you a tale of Singapore,
  Of the ladies of Old Japan.
The Second Mate's guitar will twang
  And every one must sing
While Geordie Muir o' Cambuslang
  Will gi' ye a Hielan fling: —

  O drink to the men who have Gone Ashore
    With a one-two-three — rum-tum.
  Half a dozen men on the Mess Room floor,
  Six good men on the Mess Room floor,
  Drink to the men who have Gone Ashore —
    Yo ho for a bottle o' rum!

I told the tale of Singapore
  And they laughed till the tears ran down,
So I told another (they asked for more)
  Of dear old London Town:
Then Geordie Muir, who'd been to Japan,
  He told us a tale or twa
Of a little brown woman and a big brown man
  Alone in a Jin-rick-sha: —

O drink to the men who have Gone Ashore
(I 'spect they're drinkin' some).
Half a dozen men on the Mess Room floor,
Six good men with their throats all sore
Drinkin' to the men who have Gone Ashore
(Both of 'em married — O dear, O Lor!)
Yo ho for a bottle o' rum!

William McFee

THE ISLE OF OTHERIE

It was an ancient sailor man who told the tale to
      me,
A bearded, ear-ringed mariner, who sunned him on
      the quay
Beside the white-sailed *Flying Cloud,* the ship of
      Faerie.

"Oh, maids are sweet in Dunedin, and loving in
      Bombay,
But all of them are nowt to me, for all the night and
      day
I hear my little mermaid's song and dare not turn
      away!

"It was upon a summer morn, upon the Indian
      sea,
The captain called me aft to him, and said to me,
      says he,
'We'll heave to by that island, the Isle of Otherie.

"'You'll take the longboat and the casks and seek
      fresh water, son;

We'll let the crew e'en stretch their legs and have
a little fun;
The nags are full of beans, and we'll just let the
rascals run!'

"So when we came to Otherie we backed a topsail
then;
I left the captain, cook and boy, and took my jolly
men,
I tell you, it was good to set our feet on earth again!

"Some climbed the trees and flung down nuts for
sport upon their pals,
Some turned right in and slept like dogs, with
waking intervals,
And some few grouched and cursed because they
couldn't see no gals.

"We filled our casks with water, and then I took
a walk.
I like to go a-swimming where there are none to
gawk;
But turning 'round a corner, I came upon a rock.

"There sat a youthful mermaid, all pink and white
and neat!
Her riggin' — what there was of it! — was rayther
incomplete.
She wore her own bright hair, my lad, and smiled
upon me sweet.

"I stood like one dumfoundered — until she
smiled at me.

She says, 'My merry sailor-boy!' and stretched a
hand so free.
So down I plumps to hear her sing, all by the tropic
sea.

"She combed and brushed her golden hair and
sang most sweetly there,
I sat alongside worshipful — we were a happy
pair!
Till of a sudden from the ship I heard a wrathful
blare.

"'Ahoy, there, men!' the captain cried, 'You've
had your run ashore!'
I sat like one possessed, for from the sea there
came a roar,
And, rising from the foam, I saw what haunts me
evermore!

"It was my mermaid's mother, and furious was
she!
She scolded darling daughter, and her language it
was free,
But daughter laughed and bade her hush, and
leaped into the sea.

"Before she leaped, I caught at her and kissed her
on the cheek.
She was quite plump and soft to touch, but had a
fishy reek.
But never mortal maiden's lips were half so fair to
seek!

'And that is why I never mind the girls nor dream
    of wealth,
I dream of seeking Otherie, and courting her by
    stealth!
And very glad indeed I'd be to drink your honor's
    health."

John Williams Brotherton

A SAILOR'S YARN

This is the tale that was told to me
By a battered and shattered son of the sea, —
To me and my messmate, Silas Green,
When I was a guileless young marine.

'Twas the good ship Gyascutus,
   All in the China Seas,
With the wind a-lee and the capstan free
   To catch the summer breeze.

'Twas Captain Porgie on the deck,
   To his mate in the mizzen hatch,
While the boatswain bold, in the forward hold,
   Was winding his larboard watch.

"Oh, how does our good ship head to-night?
   How heads our gallant craft?"
"Oh, she heads to the E. S. W. by N.,
   And the binnacle lies abaft!"

"Oh, what does the quadrant indicate,
   And how does the sextant stand?"

"Oh, the sextant's down to the freezing point,
   And the quadrant's lost a hand!"

"Oh, and if the quadrant has lost a hand
   And the sextant falls so low,
It's our bodies and bones to Davy Jones
   This night are bound to go!

"Oh, fly aloft to the garboard strake!
   And reef the spanker boom;
Bend a studding-sail on the martingale,
   To give her weather room.

"O boatswain, down in the for'ard hold,
   What water do you find?"
"Four foot and a half by the royal gaff
   And rather more behind!"

"O sailors, collar your marline spikes
   And each belaying-pin;
Come, stir your stumps and spike the pumps,
   Or more'll be coming in!"

They stirred their stumps, they spiked the pumps,
   They spliced the mizzen brace;
Aloft and alow they worked, but oh!
   The water gained apace.

They bored a hole above the keel,
   To let the water out;
But, strange to say, to their dismay,
   The water in did spout.

Then up spoke the Cook of our gallant ship,
    And he was a lubber brave:
"I have several wives in various ports,
    And my life I'd orter save."

Then up spoke the Captain of Marines,
    Who dearly loved his prog:
"It's awful to die, but it's worse to be dry,
    So I move we pipes to grog."

Oh, then 'twas the noble second mate,
    What filled them all with awe;
The second mate, as bad men hate,
    And cruel skippers jaw.

He took the anchor on his back
    And leaped into the main;
Through foam and spray he clove his way,
    And sunk and rose again!

Through foam and spray, a league away
    The anchor stout he bore;
Till, safe at last, he made it fast
    And warped the ship ashore!

"'Taint much of a job to talk about,
    But a ticklish thing to see,
And suthin' to do, if I say it, too,
    For that second mate was me!"

Such was the tale that was told to me
    By that modest and truthful son of the sea;

And I envy the life of a second mate,
  Though captains curse him and sailors hate,
For he ain't like some of the swabs I've seen,
  As would go and lie to a poor marine.
                    James Jeffrey Roche

A CAPITAL SHIP

A capital ship for an ocean trip
  Was the "Walloping Window-blind"!
No gale that blew dismayed her crew
  Or troubled the captain's mind;
The man at the wheel was taught to feel
  Contempt for the wildest blow,
Tho' it often appeared when the weather had
      cleared,
  That he'd been in his bunk below.

The bo'swain's mate was very sedate,
  Yet fond of amusement, too;
He played hopscotch with the starboard watch,
  While the captain tickled the crew!
And the gunner we had was apparently mad,
  For he sat on the after rail,
And fired salutes with the captain's boots,
  In the teeth of the booming gale!

The captain sat in a commodore's hat
  And dined, in a royal way,
On toasted pigs and pickles and figs
  And gummery bread each day.
But the cook was Dutch, and behaved as such;
  For the diet he gave the crew

Was a number of tons of hot cross-buns
  Chopped up with sugar and glue.

And we all felt ill as mariners will
  On a diet that's cheap and rude;
And we shivered and shook as we dipped the cook
  In a tub of his gluesome food.
Then nautical pride we laid aside,
  And we cast the vessel ashore
On the Gulliby Isles, where the Poohpooh smiles,
  And the Anagazanders roar.

Composed of sand was that favored land,
  And trimmed with cinnamon straws;
And pink and blue was the pleasing hue
  Of the Tickletoeteaser's claws.
And we sat on the edge of a sandy ledge
  And shot at the whistling bee;
And the Binnacle-bats wore waterproof hats,
  As they danced in the sounding sea.

On rubagub bark, from dawn to dark,
  We fed till we all had grown
Uncommonly shrunk, when a Chinese junk
  Came up from the Torriby Zone.
She was chubby and square, but we didn't much
    care,
  And we cheerily put to sea;
And we left the crew of the junk to chew
  On the bark of the rubagub tree.

                    Charles Edward Carryl

THE MARINES' HYMN

From the halls of Montezuma
  To the shores of Tripoli
We fight our country's battles
  On the land as on the sea.
First to fight for right and freedom
  And to keep our honor clean,
We are proud to claim the title
  Of United States Marine.

Our flag's unfurled to every breeze
  From dawn to setting sun;
We have fought in every clime or place
  . Where we could take a gun;
In the snow of far-off northern lands
  And in sunny tropic scenes
You will find us always on the job —
  The United States Marines.

Here's health to you, and to our corps,
  Which we are proud to serve;
In many a strife we have fought for life
  And never lost our nerve;
If the Army and the Navy
  Ever look on heaven's scenes
They will find the streets are guarded by
  The United States Marines.

Anonymous

THE DECKHANDS

There's some is bums from city slums
That ain't so strong on knowledge;

There's some that hails from county jails
An' some that hails from college;
There's some is mild an' some is wild
An' some is smart an' chipper —
The kind that climbs an' gets, sometimes,
To be a mate or skipper.

    A lousy lot
    You'll say, an' not
What you'd consider what is what;
    Well, yes, we lack
    A high shellac
But we're not meant for bric-a-brac.

  Believe me, pard, we're rough and hard
An' scarcely things of beauty;
We're never made for dress parade
But just for heavy duty;
To strain our spines at handlin' lines —
To do our stint of swabbin' —
When combers roll to pass the coal
To keep the screws a-throbbin'.

    It's true we ain't
    Exactly "quaint"
Like "hale old salts" the painters paint,
    But we can do
    The work for you —
An' that's the business of a crew.

  We're single guys without no ties
Of any kind to bind us,
Tho' I can't state the aggregate
Of girls we've left behind us.

In port we drink an' get in "clink"
In spite of ev'ry warnin' —
Our money spent, we're all content
To ship again next mornin'.

    The mate may "rare"
    An' swear an' tear —
Us deckhands doesn't greatly care,
    For kicks an' blame
    Is in the game —
They've got to have us just the same.

November blows an' wintry snows
Don't find us any glummer,
We still can shirk our daily work
As well as in the summer.
For, so we gets our cigarettes
An' wages, when it's over
We'll take a trip in any ship
An' think ourselves in clover.

    We wouldn't please
    At balls or teas,
Where high-toned folks is what you sees;
    But don't you doubt
    This fact, old scout,
We're guys they can't get on without.

Anonymous

THE FATE OF THE "GOOD INTENT"

(*A Volsteadian Coronach*)

It was the brave ship "Good Intent"
That sailed across the continent —

Her captain's name was Badly Bent
 Her purser's name was Broke.

O leaden-helmed and hard to steer,
 Her cargo — vain regrets and beer,
The course she laid was wild and queer,
 Her compass was a joke.

With no regard for wind or tide,
 From port to port she gaily plied —
And thus on lucky chance relied —
 And every ship she spoke;

She hailed the lugger "Do It Now,"
 She crossed the "Onward's" speeding prow,
And sunk the good old frigate "How"!
 And then went up in smoke.

Overland

RHYME OF AN ANCIENT MARINER

"I've lost me Book," the Seaman said,
And shook his doleful head.
"I've lost me Book, through accident,
Some good excuse I might invent.
But that, perhaps, you would resent,
The simple statement must content,
I've lost me Book."

"My name is Smith," the Seaman said,
"My Christian name is likewise Fred.
I'd one discharge at Amsterdam
When we came back from Surinam,

An' two, I think, from Rotterdam,
An' one, (with caution) at West Ham,
But that's not in me Book."

"It makes me wild," the Seaman said,
"Enough to punch me bally head.
I join a bloomin' timber barge
With a sky-pilot taking charge,
I slave to get a good discharge,
An' yet, direckly I'm at large,
I lose me Book."

"I have no luck," the Seaman said,
As many a grimy tear he shed.
"When I was on the *Aphrodite,*
(He made it rhyme with dynamite)
She went ashore one stormy night,
The other blokes got off all right —
I lost me Book."

"The *Belvedere* blew up," he said,
"An' all her crew was counted dead,
But I, misforchunate A–B,
Was hurled into the ragin' sea,
And everyone was killed but me;
But my loss was the worst, you see —
I lost me Book."

Anonymous

A DASH TO THE POLE

'Twas out on the Archipelago
In the region of the Horn,

Somewhere in the locks of the Equinox
   And the Tropic of Capricorn.

We bumped right into the Arctic,
   Me and me matey, John.
We was near to frizz by the slush and the slizz,
   For we hadn't our flannels on.

Who'd 'a' thought that a tried explorer
   Would start for the Pole like that,
With openwork hose and summer clo'es
   And a dinky old Panama hat?

We could see the Eskimoses,
   Far out on the ice ashore,
A-turnin' up of their noses
   At the comical clo'es we wore.

We could hear the bears on the glaciers
   A-laughing kind of amused,
An' there we stud in our seashore duds
   A-looking that shamed and confused!

The whirl-i-gig Arctic breezes
   They biffed our bark abaft,
And the ice-pack shook with our sneezes,
   (For there was a terrible draft).

"Friend John," I yells to me matey,
   "Stand ready and warp the boat!"
But I suddenly found that John was drowned,
   And me alone and afloat.

I was chilled to the heart with terror
  At the loss of me matey, John.
I was chilled to the feet, for I beg to repeat,
  That I hadn't me flannels on.

When all of a dog-goned sudden
  A peak riz over the sun.
I swear on me soul 'twas the Arctic Pole —
  Then what d'ye think I done?

Then what d'ye think I done, sir,
  When that pinnacle swung in view?
I done what a wight in a similar plight
  With a similar Pole would do.

I swung the hand of the compass
  Till straight to the South points she,
And soon I divined that the Pole was behind
  And me in the open sea.

I landed next week at Coney
  Where I hitched me bark to a post,
Then I fell in a faint from pneumony
  Which I caught on the Arctic coast —

Out there on the Archipelago,
  In the region of the Horn,
Somewhere in the locks of the Equinox
  And the Tropic of Capricorn.

And that is why in summer,
  When it's most undeniably warm,
I dresses in felt and pelican pelt,
  Which is suitable clo'es for storm.

And it's highly correct and proper
  To start for the Pole like that;
But I nevermore goes in me openwork hose
  And me dinky old Panama hat.

              Wallace Irwin

SOUTH SEA STUFF

The Copra soars above the shores
  That pearl a sapphire sea.
And, like as not, a Hottentot
  Is waiting there for me.
The bay is calm, the fronded palm
  With lithe and sinuous grace
Bends o'er the maid and steeps in shade
  Her rather shadier face.
And if she stands upon the sands
  And wears that wistful smile
Till I appear, I sort of fear
  She'll be there quite a while.

Where tabus roam their island home
  With taafas on their brows,
Or dive through coves to pluck the loaves
  From sun-baked bread-fruit boughs,
For days and days a maiden's gaze
  Is fixed upon the blue
That she may mark my white-sailed bark
  That cleaves the atoll through.
I have not met the lady yet,
  And only wish her well,
But none the less I sort of guess
  She'll wait there quite a spell.

The paruu droops o'er dusky troops
   Of aborigines,
Who wait to hail the white man's sail
   Upon the tropic seas.
They're keen to wed, so we have read,
   And when his ship arrives,
With loving hearts they'll play the parts
   Of fond and loyal wives.
But if they wait to share my fate
   Beside the creaming foam,
They'll wait in vain — I'll tell 'em plain
   I'm quite content at home!

James J. Montague

SAILOR'S CONSOLATION

One night came on a hurricane,
   The sea was mountains rolling,
When Barney Buntline turned his quid,
   And said to Billy Bowline:
"A strong nor'wester's blowing, Bill.
   Hark! Don't you hear it roar now?
Lord help them! How I pities all
   Unlucky folks on shore now.

"Foolhardy chaps that live in towns;
   What dangers they are all in,
And now lie shaking in their beds
   For fear the roof should fall in.
Poor creatures, how they envy us
   And wishes, I've a notion,
For our good luck in such a storm
   To be upon the ocean.

"And often, Bill, I have been told
   How folks are killed, and undone,
By overturns of carriages,
   By fogs and fires in London.
We know what risks all landsmen run,
   From noblemen to tailors,
Then, Bill, let us thank Providence
   That you and me are sailors."

William Pitt

FOUR DEEP-SEA TARS *AND ANOTHER*

Two sailors sat by Mona's pier,
Both strangely dressed and rather queer,
Said Number One, "What brung us here,
     By Mona?"

Said Number Two, "Me little tale
Is known to all the men who sail;
I came here steerage, in a whale,
     I'm Jonah."

Said Number One to Number Two,
"My job's collecting for a zoo,
The gnat, the elephant, the gnu,
     The boa;

"The ape, the adder, and the skunk,
All shared me meals, all shared me bunk,
I swum ashore when I was drunk,
     I'm Noah."

As these two freaks thus voiced their woe
Beside them suddenly arose,

A third one, who, instead of clothes,
        Had hair on:

Said he: "You know you're both in wrong,
And now you've sung your little song,
I'll take you back where you belong,
        I'm Charon."

But as they swam toward the boat,
A fourth appeared who got their "goat,"
No trousers wore he, nor a coat —
        Nor had 'em:

"Good even'n, friends," said he in glee,
"Looks like you're off upon a spree,
I hope you've not forgotten me,
        I'm Adam."

A flash then burst upon the scene,
A shape with teeth and fearsome mien,
Who, while he made the boat careen,
        Cried "Steady!

"I am not dead, nor wish to die,
You shall not let this thing get by
Without my finger in the pie,
        I'm Teddy!"

                  Anonymous

A SEA-GOING RUBAIYAT

In eastern port, 'ere muezzin's call to prayer,
The Captain Omar, he of scatt'ring hair,

While the good ship at her moorings strains and
    stresses,
Calls the Black Gang and them thus addresses:

"Oh, greasy servants of the mighty genii Steam,
To true believers like myself, unclean!
I, and me, myself, shall take thee home;
Be calm! Thou shalt not sleep beneath the foam!

"By Banka Strait, where buoys go astray,
And make the cautious captain lose his way,
Where wooded islands rise from out the deep,
I'm watchful still when other *hombres* sleep.

"Fear not the crashing seas nor surges' boom!
No rock shall ever enter engine room,
Tho' deep beneath the wave fear not thy fate —
By Noah's method I will navigate.

"What if some liars say he drifted 'round
For forty days, then ran the ark aground —
Tho' Allah swore it, would I not believe!
One's never wrong if Sounding-lead he heave.

"In river, bay, in straits or open sea,
The sun may shine or not for all of me.
My mates take sight and when all three have done,
I take a sounding and ignore the sun.

"For modern methods care I not a whit —
My mates may tear their hair or throw a fit;
The Sounding-lead was Captain Noah's rule
And I'm of Noah's Navigation School.

"So dive in bilge if so it be Thou must!
Pour on plunging rod and groaning thrust!
By the beard of Moses! thou art safe my men —
For I, myself, will take thee home again.

"Keep but the fire of life within the boilers,
My engineers, my wipers and my oilers,
And shining dollars shall be thy reward
From the Protector of the Poor, my Shipping
      Board."

William Francis Roantree

WHAT HO! SHE BLOWS!

Yes, I am the bloke what shovelled the coke
  On the whaler, Lally-ma-Loo;
And the gallant soul what scuttled the coal
  Is the same that's talking to you.

We stud in the bight that starry night
  A-tacking agin the gale
When the Capting shouts, "She spins, she spouts!
  Yo-ho and avast, the whale!"

(Of course, you know that the yell "Yo-ho!"
  Should mean, "Slack stidder and cast!"
And you understand the simple command
  When the Capting hollers, "Avast!")

So we on with our coats and we manned the boats
  For the point where the whale she blew,
And we carried aboard a bundle o' cord,
  A pearl-handled knife and a screw.

"O Capting Nye," I says, says I,
  "Now what are we going to do,
In such a gale to murder a whale
  With a pearl-handled knife and a screw?"

But the Capting's gaze was over the haze
  And never a word spoke he,
And never a speech and never a screech,
  And never a word to me.

Till he says and he said as he p'inted ahead,
  Right straight at the monster's fin,
"His actions denote that his heart's in his throat,
  So jab him under the chin!"

So he held the screw — I'm a-tellin' you true —
  And he handed the knife to me;
And gripping the sheath in me wisdom teeth
  I plumped straight into the sea.

Yes, out I clumb and over I swum
  Right under the monster's fin,
Where I opens me knife, and regardless of life,
  I jabs him under the chin.

Then the whale piped high a leviathan cry
  And he guggled in huge despair;
Then he splattered our sail and stud on his tail
  And turned nine flips in the air.

"My eye, my eye!" says Capting Nye,
  "I didn't expect that there,
That a full sized whale would stand on his tail
  And turn nine flips in the air."

And he says, says he, "It appears to me,
  That the animal must be vexed.
We'd better be going, — there isn't no knowing
  What he will be doing next."

So we switched our tack and we hurried back
  To the jolly old Lally-ma-Loo,
Me holding the cord which we had aboard
  And the Capting holding the screw.

And he says to me, "If a way there be
  To murder a whale in a storm —
It's to bandage his eyes and smother his cries
  With a bottle o' chloroform."

Wallace Irwin

THE BEACH-COMBER

I'd like to return to the world again,
To the dutiful, work-a-day world of men, —
For I'm sick of the beach-comber's lazy lot,
Of the one volcano flaming hot,
With the snow 'round its edge and the fire in its
        throat,
And this tropical island that seems a-float
Like a world set in space all alone in the sea. . . .
How I wish that a ship, it would stop for me.
I'm sick of the brown girl that loves me, I'm sick
Of the cocoanut groves, — you can't take me too
        quick
From this place, though it's rich in all nature can
        give . . .
For I want to return where it's harder to live,

Where men struggle for life, where they work and
    find sweet
Their rest after toil, and the food that they eat . . .
What? A ship's in the offing? . . . dear God, let me
    hide, —
They're in need of a sailor, are waiting the tide
To put off? . . . I will hide where the great cliff
    hangs sheer —
Give 'em mangoes and goats, *and don't tell 'em
    I'm here!*

Harry Kemp

BALLAD OF THE NEW FIGUREHEAD

As I sailed down the Zuyder Zee,
    (*Oho, my lads, just pipe your eye!*)
The waves were high, the sails were free,
The wind was shrill and roared with glee,
And an adventure came to me.
    (*Now take my word or leave it!*)

Our Figurehead to life awoke —
    (*Oho, my lads, look sharp ahead!*)
Now she was made of quartered oak,
And you may think it all a joke,
But, mercy me! She up and spoke!
    (*Now take my word or leave it!*)

Said she, "Look here, my worthy mate —
    (*Oho, my lads, just pass the grog!*)
My make-up is 'way out of date.
I want silk hose — my size is 8 —
And three-strapped sandals, black and slate!
    (*Now take my word or leave it!*)

"Remove from me this lengthy gown —
  (*Oho, my lads, now port your helm!*)
It makes me look like a circus clown,
I wish the shortest skirt in town;
So look alive! Don't make it brown!
  (*Now take my word or leave it!*)

"I want a wrist-watch too," she said
  (*Oho, my lads, now starboard, there!*)
"Tuxedo sweater, good and red!
And listen here — don't be misled —
The Shetland kind with wide-mesh spread!
  (*Now take my word or leave it!*)

"I wish ear-pendants — get a pair —
  (*Oho, my lads, now take a reef!*)
And don't you ever, ever dare
To gild again this waist-length hair!
I want it bobbed at once, so there!
  (*Now take my word or leave it!*)

"A lip-stick, too, I wish you'd get —
  (*Oho, my lads, just heave the lead!*)
I want some rouge that stands the wet,
And powder — lots of it, you bet!
And one thing more — a cigarette!"
  (*Now take my word or leave it!*)

I sailed back up the Zuyder Zee
  (*Oho, my lads, the anchor weigh!*)
I hardly knew that I was me,
So sort o' seashell-shocked, you see —
The Figurehead, she winked at me!
  (*Now take my word or leave it!*)
                    Blanche Elizabeth Wade

THE "LEVIATHAN'S" THREE HUNDRED

Down the bay, down the bay,
Down the bay onward,
To Cuba and Panama
   Sailed the three hundred.
"Bring up the lemonade!
We're sailin' dry!" he said.
Down to Guantanamo
   Sailed the three hundred.

"Bring up the lemonade!"
Was there a man dismayed?
Not though each lubber thought
Volstead had blundered.
Their's not to make reply,
Their's not to reason why,
Their's but to travel dry.
Down to Guantanamo
   Sailed the three hundred.

Taxpayers near to them,
Taxpayers far from them,
Taxpayers after them,
   Grumbled and thundered.
Stormed at with printer's ink,
Yet not a man did shrink,
Off to the Antilles,
Off to the Land of Drink
   Sailed the three hundred.

Flushed were their faces there,
Flushed in the tropic air;

They made wine-cellars bare,
Drinking Bacardi while
  All Cuba wondered.
Each with a dollar smoke
Thought it a merry joke
If Uncle Sam he broke.
Then they sailed back — the bunch,
  All the three hundred.

Taxpayers near to them,
Taxpayers far from them,
Taxpayers facing them
  Grumbled and thundered.
Stormed at with printer's ink
They who would never shrink
Came from Guantanamo,
Left Cuba on the blink —
All that was left of it
  By the three hundred.

When can their glory fade?
"How can the bills be paid?"
  Poor Mellon wondered.
Oh, the joy ride they made,
With Chairman Lasker's aid,
  Famous three hundred.

Anonymous

THE LANDLUBBER'S TOAST

'Tis pleasant to taste of the spray
As the waters dash over the rail
  To be frozen and wet
  And extremely upset

In the teeth of a thundering gale.
But the joys of a seafaring life
Are naught but the emptiest boast,
   As glasses we clink
   In a room that can't sink
   And delightedly drink
A new toast:
   "Oh, here's to the land, yo ho!
   Drain, drain every foaming tankard,
     Oh, here's to the sea
     As it looks to me
   From a beach that is firmly anchored.
     Oh, here's to the quiet, respectable street
     Where the winds never howl and the waves
      never beat,
     Where the ground has been trained to stick
      close to your feet, —
   A health to the land, yo ho!"

There's a charm in the mariner's life,
Of pleasure he suffers no lack,
   As he tumbles through space
   The winds slap his face
And the boom makes a dent in his back.
When the waves wash him over the side
In a playful and innocent style,
   The fishes who note
   His descent from the boat
   Eat him up, table d'hôte,
With a smile.
   "So here's to the land, yo ho!
   Drain, drain every tankard foaming;
     The delights I resign

Of the billowy brine —
Let others do all my roaming.
Oh, here's to the land where you stick to your
chairs,
Where the beds do not fire you out unawares,
Where you know which is down, and which is
up-stairs —
A health to the land, yo ho!"

Thomas R. Ybarra

TEN THOUSAND MILES AWAY

It's ho! for a gay and a gallant bark,
A brisk and a rattling breeze,
A gallant crew and a captain, too,
To carry me o'er the seas —
To carry me o'er the seas, my boys,
To my own true love so gay —
For taking a trip in a Government ship
Ten thousand miles away.

(*Chorus*)

And it's blow, ye winds heigh-ho,
It's a-roaming I will go —
I'll stay no more on England's shore,
So let your music play.
For I am off on the morning train
To cross the raging main —
I am on the rove to my own true love
Ten thousand miles away.

My true love she is beautiful —
My true love she is fair;

Her eyes are blue as the violet's hue
And crimson is her hair;
And crimson is her hair, my boys —
And while I sing this lay,
She is doing the grand in a distant land
Ten thousand miles away.

(*Chorus*)

Dark and dismal was the day
When last I saw my Meg;
She had a Government band around each hand
And one around each leg —
And one around each leg, my boys,
All dressed in a suit of gray —
Oh, my love says she'll remember me
Ten thousand miles away.

(*Chorus*)

I wish I were a bo's'n tight
Or e'en a bombardier —
I'd hurry afloat in an open boat
And to my true love steer;
And to my true love steer, my boys,
Where the laughing dolphins play —
Where the shrimps and sharks are having their
larks
Ten thousand miles away.

(*Chorus*)

The sun may shine in the London fog
And the river Thames run clear;

The ocean brine may turn to wine,
And I might forget my beer.
I might forget my beer, my boys,
And the landlord's quarter day —
But I'll never forget my own sweetheart
Ten thousand miles away.

(*Chorus*)

Anonymous

SAILORS' CHANTEYS

LONG DRAG

A Long Time Ago
Blow, Boys, Blow
Blow the Man Down
Boney Was a Warrior
Dead Horse
Hanging Johnnie

Leave Her, Johnny, Leave Her
Reuben Ranzo
Roll the Cotton Down
Tom's Gone to Ilo
Whisky for my Johnnie

SHORT DRAG

Haul Away, Joe
Haul the Bowline

Johnny Boker
Paddy Doyle

CAPSTAN

Homeward Bound
Hoodah-Day
The Plains of Mexico

Rio Grande
Sally Brown
We're All Bound to Go

The Wide Missouri

PUMPING

One More Day

Storm-Along

OLD SEA SONGS

A-Roving
Farewell, and Adieu to You

Rolling Home
High Barbaree
The Golden Vanity

A LONG TIME AGO

With swing

A long time and a ver-y long time,

To me way-ha - ha - ya! A long time and a

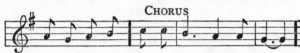

ver - y long time, And a long time a - go.

Solo   A dollar a day is a stevedore's pay,
Chorus   To me way-ha-ha-yah!
Solo   A dollar a day, I heard them say,
Chorus   And a long time ago.

Solo   I bought in Hong Kong a pretty silk dress,
Chorus   To me way-ha-ha-yah!
Solo   I'm taking it home to my sweetheart Bess,
Chorus   And a long time ago.

Solo   My Bess is fair and sweet to view,
Chorus   To me way-ha-ha-yah!
Solo   Her hair is brown and her eyes are blue,
Chorus   And a long time ago.

Solo   I thought I heard our second mate say,
Chorus   To me way-ha-ha-yah!
Solo   One more pull and then belay,
Chorus   And a long time ago.

BLOW, BOYS, BLOW

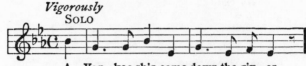

A Yan-kee ship came down the riv-er,

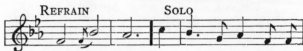

Blow, boys, blow! A Yan-kee ship and a

Yan-kee skipper, Blow, my bul-ly boys, blow!

Solo   A Yankee ship on the Congo river,
Refrain   Blow, boys, blow!
Solo   Her masts they bend and her sails they
                 shiver,
Refrain   Blow, my bully boys, blow!

Solo   How do you know she's a Yankee clipper?
Refrain   Blow, boys, blow!
Solo   The Stars and Stripes they fly above her,
Refrain   Blow, my bully boys, blow!

Solo   Who do you think is captain of her?
Refrain   Blow, boys, blow!
Solo   Old Holy Joe, the darky lover,
Refrain   Blow, my bully boys, blow!

Solo   What do you think she's got for cargo?
Refrain   Blow, boys, blow!

Solo   Old shot and shell, she breaks the em-
            bargo,
Refrain Blow, my bully boys, blow!

Solo   What do you think they have for dinner?
Refrain Blow, boys, blow!
Solo   Hot water soup, but slightly thinner,
Refrain Blow, my bully boys, blow!

Solo   Oh, blow today and blow tomorrow,
Refrain Blow, boys, blow!
Solo   And blow for all old tars in sorrow,
Refrain Blow, my bully boys, blow!

BLOW THE MAN DOWN

Oh, blow the man down, bul-lies, Knock him right

down,   Way - - ay, blow the man down!

Oh, blow the man down, bullies, Knock him right down,

Give me some time to blow the man down.

Solo   As I was a-walking down Paradise street,
Chorus   To my aye, aye, blow the man down!
Solo   A brass-bound policeman, I chanced for to meet,
Chorus   Give me some time to blow the man down.

Solo   I hailed him in English and hailed him all 'round,
Chorus   To my aye, aye, blow the man down!
Solo   Ship ahoy! ship ahoy! Oh, where are you bound?
Chorus   Give me some time to blow the man down.

Solo   A-watching the damsels so gay and so young,
Chorus   To my aye, aye, blow the man down!
Solo   It's arm-in-arm we strolled 'round the town,
Chorus   Give me some time to blow the man down.

Solo   Oh, policeman, policeman, please come along,
Chorus   To my aye, aye, blow the man down!
Solo   I'm a flying-fish sailor, just home from Hong Kong,
Chorus   Give me some time to blow the man down.

Solo   There was an old skipper, I don't know his name,

Chorus   To my aye, aye, blow the man down;

Solo   Although he once played a remarkable game,

Chorus   Give me some time to blow the man down.

Solo   For his ship lay becalmed in the tropical seas,

Chorus   To my aye, aye, blow the man down;

Solo   And he whistled all day, but in vain, for a breeze,

Chorus   Give me some time to blow the man down.

Solo   But a seal heard his whistle and loudly did call,

Chorus   To my aye, aye, blow the man down;

Solo   "Roll up your white canvas, jib, spanker and all,"

Chorus   Give me some time to blow the man down.

BONEY WAS A WARRIOR

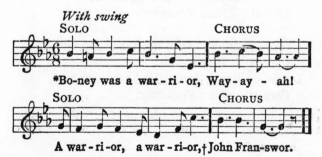

With swing

SOLO ... CHORUS

*Bo-ney was a war-ri-or, Way-ay - ah!

SOLO ... CHORUS

A war-ri-or, a war-ri-or,† John Fran-swor.

* "Boney" refers to Napoleon Bonaparte.

† "John Franswor" is a corruption of Jean Francois.

Solo   Boney beat the Prussians,
Chorus   Way-ay, ah!
Solo   Then he whipped the Russians,
Chorus   John Franswor.

Solo   Boney went to Waterloo,
Chorus   Way-ay, ah!
Solo   Boney went to Waterloo,
Chorus   John Franswor.

Solo   Boney met a warrior,
Chorus   Way-ay, ah!
Solo   Boney met a warrior,
Chorus   John Franswor.

Solo   Boney was a prisoner,
Chorus   Way-ay, ah!
Solo   Boney was a prisoner,
Chorus   John Franswor.

Solo   He was sent to St. Helena,
Chorus   Way-ay, ah!
Solo   There he was a prisoner,
Chorus   John Franswor.

Solo   Boney broke his heart and died,
Chorus   Way-ay, ah!
Solo   Boney broke his heart and died,
Chorus   John Franswor.

DEAD HORSE

Slow

Poor old man, your horse is going to die,

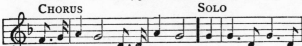

And I say so, and I hope so; Oh, poor old man, your

horse is going to die, Oh, poor old man.

Solo	For ninety days I've ridden on him,
Chorus	And I say so, and I hope so;
Solo	When he dies I'll tan his skin.
Chorus	Oh, poor old man.

Solo	If he lives we'll ride him again,
Chorus	And I say so, and I hope so;
Solo	We'll ride him again with a tighter rein,
Chorus	Oh, poor old man.

Solo	It's up aloft the horse must go,
Chorus	And I say so, and I hope so;
Solo	We'll hoist him up, then bury him low,
Chorus	Oh, poor old man.

Solo	We'll hoist him to the mainyard-arm,
Chorus	And I say so, and I hope so,

Solo   We'll hoist him to the mainyard-arm,
Chorus   Oh, poor old man.

Solo   Then drop him to the depths of the sea,
Chorus   And I say so, and I hope so,
Solo   Then drop him to the depths of the sea,
Chorus   Oh, poor old man.

HANGING JOHNNIE

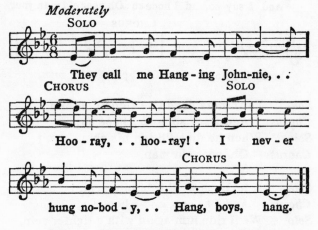

Moderately

SOLO

They call me Hang-ing John-nie, . .

CHORUS   SOLO

Hoo-ray, . . hoo-ray! . I nev-er

CHORUS

hung no-bod-y, . . Hang, boys, hang.

Solo   They say I hung my mother,
Chorus   Hooray, hooray!
Solo   And then I hung my brother,
Chorus   Hang, boys, hang.

Solo   They say I hung for money,
Chorus   Hooray, hooray!
Solo   They say I am so funny,
Chorus   Hang, boys, hang.

Solo   They say I hung a robber,
Chorus   Hooray, hooray!
Solo   They say I hung a robber,
Chorus   Hang, boys, hang.

Solo   Let's haul and hang together,
Chorus   Hooray, hooray!
Solo   And hang for better weather,
Chorus   Hang, boys, hang.

LEAVE HER, JOHNNY, LEAVE HER

Moderately

Oh, the times are hard and the wa-ges low,

Leave her, John-ny, leave her! I'll pack my bag and

go be-low; It's time for us to leave her.

Solo   It's growl you may but go you must,
Chorus   Leave her, Johnny, leave her!
Solo   It matters not whether you're last or first,
Chorus   It's time for us to leave her.

Solo   I'm getting thin and growing sad,
Chorus   Leave her, Johnny, leave her!
Solo   Since first I joined this wooden-clad,
Chorus   It's time for us to leave her.

Solo I thought I heard the second-mate say
Chorus "Leave her, Johnny, leave her!
Solo Just one more drag and then belay,
Chorus It's time for us to leave her."

Solo The work was hard, the voyage long,
Chorus Leave her, Johnny, leave her!
Solo The seas were high, the gales were strong,
Chorus It's time for us to leave her.

Solo The sails are furled, our work is done,
Chorus Leave her, Johnny, leave her!
Solo And now on shore, we'll have our fun,
Chorus It's time for us to leave her.

REUBEN RANZO

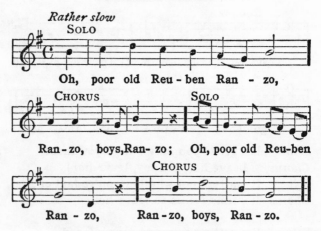

Oh, poor old Reu-ben Ran-zo,
Ran-zo, boys, Ran-zo; Oh, poor old Reu-ben
Ran-zo, Ran-zo, boys, Ran-zo.

Solo Ranzo was no sailor,
Chorus Ranzo, boy, Ranzo!

Solo   He shipped on board a whaler,
Chorus   Ranzo, boys, Ranzo!

Solo   Ranzo joined the "Beauty,"
Chorus   Ranzo, boys, Ranzo!
Solo   He could not do his duty,
Chorus   Ranzo, boys, Ranzo!

Solo   The skipper was a dandy,
Chorus   Ranzo, boys, Ranzo!
Solo   He was too fond of brandy,
Chorus   Ranzo, boys, Ranzo!

Solo   He called Ranzo a lubber,
Chorus   Ranzo, boys, Ranzo!
Solo   And made him eat whale blubber,
Chorus   Ranzo, boys, Ranzo!

Solo   They set him holy-stoning,
Chorus   Ranzo, boys, Ranzo!
Solo   And cared not for his groaning,
Chorus   Ranzo, boys, Ranzo!

Solo   Ranzo now is skipper,
Chorus   Ranzo, boys, Ranzo!
Solo   Of a China Clipper,
Chorus   Poor old Reuben Ranzo!

ROLL THE COTTON DOWN

Oh, roll the cot - ton, roll it down,

Oh, roll the cot-ton down; Oh, roll the cot - ton,

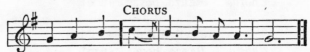

roll it down, Oh, roll the cot-ton down.

Solo   I thought I heard our old man say,
Chorus   Oh, roll the cotton down!
Solo   He'd sail away to Mobile Bay,
Chorus   Oh, roll the cotton down!

Solo   I heard him say to Mobile Bay,
Chorus   Oh, roll the cotton down!
Solo   He'd sail away at break of day,
Chorus   Oh, roll the cotton down!

Solo   Mobile Bay is no place for me,
Chorus   Oh, roll the cotton down!
Solo   I'll sail away on some other sea,
Chorus   Oh, roll the cotton down!

TOM'S GONE TO ILO

Rather slow

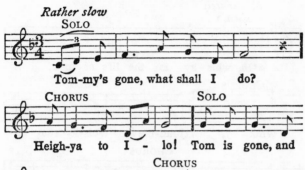

Tom-my's gone, what shall I do?

Heigh-ya to I - lo! Tom is gone, and

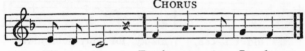

I'll go too.   Tom's gone to I - lo.

Solo	He's gone away to Ilo Bay,
Chorus	Heigh-ya to Ilo!
Solo	To Ilo Bay I heard him say,
Chorus	Tom's gone to Ilo.
Solo	Way 'round to Callao,
Chorus	Heigh-ya to Ilo!
Solo	Those Spanish girls he'll see, I know,
Chorus	Tom's gone to Ilo.
Solo	Oh, I love Tom and he loves me,
Chorus	Heigh-ya to Ilo!
Solo	He thinks of me, when out at sea,
Chorus	Tom's gone to Ilo.
Solo	Tommy's gone forever more,
Chorus	Heigh-ya to Ilo!
Solo	I'll never see my Tom no more,
Chorus	Tom's gone to Ilo.

WHISKY FOR MY JOHNNIE

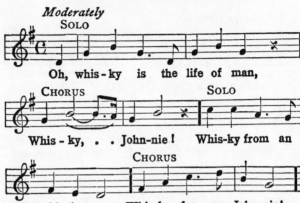

Moderately

SOLO

Oh, whis-ky is the life of man,

CHORUS   SOLO

Whis-ky, . . John-nie! Whis-ky from an

CHORUS

old tin can, Whis-ky for my John-nie!

Solo	Whisky makes me pawn my clothes,
Chorus	Whisky, Johnnie!
Solo	Whisky gave me a broken nose,
Chorus	Whisky for my Johnnie!
Solo	Whisky makes me feel so sad,
Chorus	Whisky, Johnnie!
Solo	Whisky killed my poor old Dad,
Chorus	Whisky for my Johnnie!
Solo	Whisky took my brains away,
Chorus	Whisky, Johnnie!
Solo	One more pull, and then belay,
Chorus	Whisky for my Johnnie!

HAUL AWAY, JOE

With swing

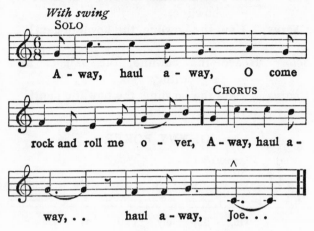

A - way, haul a - way, O come rock and roll me o - ver, A - way, haul a - way, . . haul a - way, Joe. . .

Solo   Oh, once I courted an Irish girl, and she
was fat and lazy,

Chorus   Away, haul away, haul away, Joe!

Solo   But now I'm courting a yellow girl, she
drives me almost crazy,

Chorus   Away, haul away, haul away, Joe!

HAUL THE BOWLINE

Vigorously

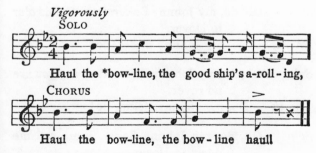

Haul the *bow-line, the good ship's a-roll-ing,
Haul the bow-line, the bow-line haul!

* A small rope on the leach of a square-sail to steady it.

Solo   Heave the bowline, the fore- and main-top
                 bowline,
Chorus   Haul the bowline, the bowline haul!

Solo   Heave the bowline, the skipper he's
                 a-growling,
Chorus   Haul the bowline, the bowline haul!

JOHNNY BOKER

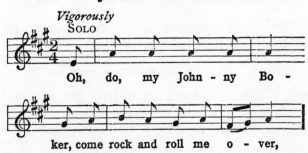

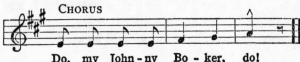

Solo   Oh, do, my Johnny Boker, from Calais o'er
                 to Dover,
Chorus   Do, my Johnny Boker, do!

Solo   Oh, do, my Johnny Boker, they say you are
                 no rover,
Chorus   Do, my Johnny Boker, do!

Solo   Oh, do, my Johnny Boker, come roll me
                 down to Dover,
Chorus   Do, my Johnny Boker, do!

*PADDY DOYLE

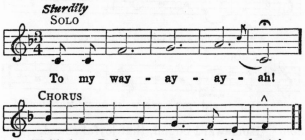

Sturdily

SOLO

To my way - ay - ay - ah!

CHORUS

We'll hang Pad - dy Doyle for his boots!

We'll tauten the bunt and we'll furl and —
We'll hang Paddy Doyle for his boots!

We'll bunt up the sail with a fling and —
We'll hang Paddy Doyle for his boots!

HOMEWARD BOUND

Moderately

SOLO

We're homeward bound to   Bos - ton town,

CHORUS

Good-by, fare you well, good-by, fare you well.

* Sung aloft in smothering sail and tossing the bunt on the yard.

We're homeward bound with su-gar and rum.

Hur - rah! my boys, we're home-ward bound.

Solo   Homeward bound, that joyful sound,

Chorus   Good-by, fare you well, good-by, fare you well,

Solo   We'll heave on the capstan and make it spin round,

Chorus   Hurrah! my boys, we're homeward bound.

Solo   Homeward bound, and our sails we will set,

Chorus   Good-by, fare you well, good-by, fare you well,

Solo   Good-by to the girls on the pier with regret,

Chorus   Hurrah! my boys, we're homeward bound.

HOODAH-DAY

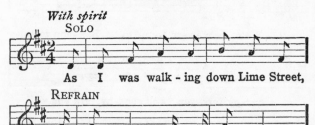

As I was walk - ing down Lime Street,

A hoo - dah, and a hoo - day!

A charm-ing maid I chanced to meet,

And a hoodah, hoo-dah-day! Blow, boys, blow, for

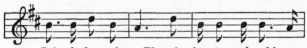

Cal - i - for - ni - o, There's plen-ty of gold, so

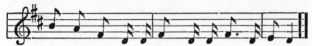

I've been told, On the banks of the Sa-cra-men-to.

Solo   This maid was neat and fair to view,
Refrain A hoodah, and a hooday!
Solo   Her hair was brown and her eyes were
               blue,
Refrain And a hoodah, hoodah-day!
Chorus   Blow, boys, blow, etc.

Solo   I asked her if she'd take a trip,
Refrain A hoodah, and a hooday!
Solo   Down to the wharf to see my ship,
Refrain And a hoodah, hoodah-day!
Chorus   Blow, boys, blow, etc.

Solo   She said, "I have a sweetheart true,"
Refrain A hoodah, and a hooday!
Solo   "And I will not leave him now for you,"
Refrain And a hoodah, hoodah-day!
Chorus   Blow, boys, blow, etc.

THE PLAINS OF MEXICO

Slow

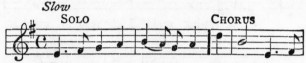

*San-ta An-na gain'd the day, Hoo-ray, San-ta

An-na! He gain'd the day, I hear them say

All a-long the plains of Mex-i-co.

Solo	Santa Anna fought for fame,
Chorus	Hooray, Santa Anna!
Solo	He fought for fame and gained his name
Chorus	All along the plains of Mexico.

Solo	It was a fierce and awful strife,
Chorus	Hooray, Santa Anna!
Solo	He met the foe and fought for life,
Chorus	All along the plains of Mexico.

RIO GRANDE

Moderately

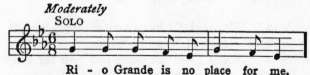

Ri - o Grande is no place for me,

* Pronounced by sailors *Santiana*, a chantey commemorating the President of Mexico during the war with the United States.

Refrain A-way .. Ri - o! .. Solo I'll pack my bag and
go to sea For we're bound to Ri - o Grande.
Chorus And a - way . . . Ri - o, . . a -
way .. Ri - o, .. Sing fare you well, my
bon-ny young lass, For we're bound to Ri-o Grande.

Solo The anchor is weighed and the sails they are set,

Refrain Away Rio!

Solo The girls that we're leaving we'll never forget,

Refrain For we're bound to Rio Grande.

Chorus And away Rio, etc.

Solo So, good-by, fair ladies we know in this town,

Refrain Away Rio!

Solo We've left you enough to buy a silk gown,

Refrain For we're bound to Rio Grande.

Chorus And away Rio, etc.

Solo   We've a ship stout and strong, and a jolly good crew,

Refrain   Away Rio!

Solo   A brass-knuckled mate, and a rough skipper too,

Refrain   For we're bound to Rio Grande.

Chorus   And away Rio, etc.

SALLY BROWN

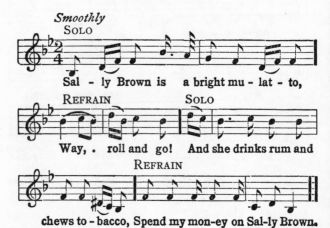

Smoothly

SOLO: Sal - ly Brown is a bright mu - lat - to,

REFRAIN: Way, . roll and go!

SOLO: And she drinks rum and chews to - bacco,

REFRAIN: Spend my mon-ey on Sal-ly Brown.

Solo   Sally Brown she's a Creole lady,

Refrain   Way, roll and go!

Solo   She's the mother of a negro baby,

Refrain   Spend my money on Sally Brown.

Solo   Seven long years I courted Sally,

Refrain   Way, roll and go!

Solo   The sweetest flower in the valley,

Refrain   Spend my money on Sally Brown.

Solo   Seven long years, and she wouldn't marry,
Refrain   Way, roll and go!
Solo   So I'll away, I will not tarry,
Refrain   Spend my money on Sally Brown.

Solo   Now my troubles they're all over,
Refrain   Way, roll and go!
Solo   She is married to a negro soldier,
Refrain   Spend my money on Sally Brown.

* WE'RE ALL BOUND TO GO

Rather slow

One morn-ing as I ram-bled A-
long the Clar-ence dock, Heave a - way, . my
John-nies, heave a - way! . . . . .
I saw a fair young dam - sel Con -

* This chantey had its origin in the days of Mr. Tapscott's packet-ships in the North Atlantic, about 1850.

vers-ing with old Tap-scott,And a - way, my

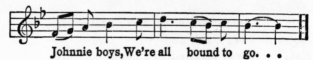

Johnnie boys,We're all   bound to go. . .

Solo   "Good morning, Mr. Tapscott,"
         "Good morning, fair maid," said he,
Chorus Heave away, my Johnnies, heave away!
Solo   "Have you got a packet-ship
         To carry me 'cross the sea?"
Chorus And away, my Johnnie boys,
              We're all bound to go.

Solo   "Oh, yes I have a clipper ship,
         The Henry Clay is her name";
Chorus Heave away, my Johnnies, heave away!
Solo   "She sails away at break of day,
         A ship of greatest fame."
Chorus And away, my Johnnie boys,
              We're all bound to go.

Solo   She sails away at break of day,
         So let your voices ring,
Chorus Heave away, my Johnnies, heave away!
Solo   For old Tapscott and his packet-ship,
         We'll shout and we will sing,
Chorus And away, my Johnnie boys,
              We're all bound to go.

THE WIDE MISSOURI
or Shenandoah

Oh,*Shan-ny-dore, I love your daughter,

A-way, my roll-ing riv-er! It's full ten

years since first I sought her. Ha, ha, .. we're

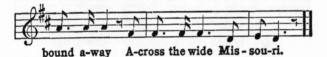

bound a-way A-cross the wide Mis-sou-ri.

Solo   Oh, Shannydore, she took my fancy,
Refrain   Away, my rolling river!
Solo   Oh, Shannydore, I love your Nancy.
Chorus   Ha, ha, we're bound away
      Across the wide Missouri.

Solo   Oh, Shannydore, I love her dearly,
Refrain   Away, my rolling river!
Solo   I'll work for her and pay you yearly.
Chorus   Ha, ha, we're bound away
      Across the wide Missouri.

* Shenandoah.

Solo   Oh, Shannydore, your good wife, Carrie,
Refrain   Away, my rolling river!
Solo   She says your daughter I may marry.
Chorus   Ha, ha, we're bound away
              Across the wide Missouri.

Solo   Oh, Shannydore, I love your daughter,
Refrain   Away, my rolling river!
Solo   I'll take her across the stormy water.
Chorus   Ha, ha, we're bound away
              Across the wide Missouri.

ONE MORE DAY

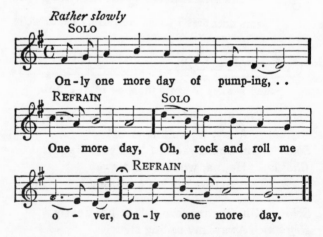

Rather slowly

On - ly one more day of pump-ing, . .

One more day, Oh, rock and roll me

o - ver, On - ly one more day.

Solo   Only one more day a-reefing,
Refrain   One more day;
Solo   Oh, rock and roll me over,
Refrain   Only one more day.

Solo	Only one more day a-sailing,
Refrain	One more day;
Solo	Oh, rock and roll me over,
Refrain	Only one more day.

Solo	Only one more day a-working,
Refrain	One more day;
Solo	Oh, rock and roll me over,
Refrain	Only one more day.

Solo	Only one more day a-furling,
Refrain	One more day;
Solo	Oh, rock and roll me over,
Refrain	Only one more day.

Solo	Only one more day a-hauling,
Refrain	One more day;
Solo	Oh, rock and roll me over,
Refrain	Only one more day.

Solo	Only one more day a-growling,
Refrain	One more day;
Solo	Oh, rock and roll me over,
Refrain	Only one more day.

Solo	Only one more day a-rolling,
Refrain	One more day;
Solo	Oh, rock and roll me over,
Refrain	Only one more day.

STORM-ALONG

Slow

SOLO

Storm - y's gone, that good old man,

CHORUS

To my way - ya, Storm - a - long;

SOLO

O Storm-y's gone, that good old man,

CHORUS

To my aye, aye, aye, Mis-ter Storm-a-long.

Solo   We'll dig his grave with a silver spade,
Chorus   To my way-ya, Storm-along;
Solo   Of the finest silk his shroud will be made,
Chorus   To my aye, aye, aye, Mister Storm-
            along.

Solo   We'll lower him down with a golden chain,
Chorus   To my way-ya, Storm-along;
Solo   Our eyes are dim but not with rain,
Chorus   To my aye, aye, aye, Mister Storm-
            along.

Solo A good old skipper to his crew,
Chorus To my way-ya, Storm-along;
Solo An able sailor brave and true,
Chorus To my aye, aye, aye, Mister Storm-along.

Solo He's moored at last and furled his sail,
Chorus To my way-ya, Storm-along;
Solo All free from wrecks and far from gales,
Chorus To my aye, aye, aye, Mister Storm-along.

Solo Old Stormy he's heard the bugle call,
Chorus To my way-ya, Storm-along;
Solo So sing his dirge now, one and all,
Chorus To my aye, aye, aye, Mister Storm-along.

A-ROVING

Lively
SOLO

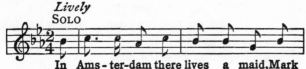

In Ams-ter-dam there lives a maid, Mark

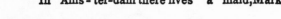

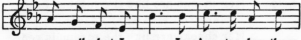

you well what I say, In Am-ster-dam there

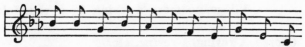

lives a maid, And she is mis-tress of her trade,

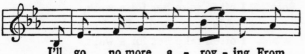

I'll go no more a - rov - ing From

CHORUS

you, fair maid. A - rov - ing, a - rov - ing,

Since rov - ing's been my ru - in, I'll

go no more a - rov-ing From you, fair maid.

Solo   Her eyes are like two stars so bright,
       Mark you well what I say!
      Her eyes are like two stars so bright,
      Her face is fair, her step is light;
      I'll go no more a-roving from you, fair
        maid.

Chorus A-roving, a-roving, etc.

Solo   Her cheeks are like the rosebuds red,
       Mark you well what I say!
      Her cheeks are like the rosebuds red,
      There's wealth of hair upon her head;
      I'll go no more a-roving from you, fair
        maid.

Chorus A-roving, a-roving, etc.

Solo   I often take her for a walk,
       Mark you well what I say!
      I often take her for a walk,

And love to hear her merry talk;
I'll go no more a-roving from you, fair
    maid.

Chorus A-roving, a-roving, etc.

Solo I love this fair maid as my life,
    Mark you well what I say!
I love this fair maid as my life,
And soon she'll be my little wife;
I'll go no more a-roving from you, fair
    maid.

Chorus A-roving, a-roving, etc.

Solo And if you'd know this maiden's name,
    Mark you well what I say!
And if you'd know this maiden's name,
Why soon like mine, 'twill be the same;
I'll go no more a-roving from you, fair
    maid.

Chorus A-roving, a-roving, etc.

FAREWELL AND ADIEU TO YOU

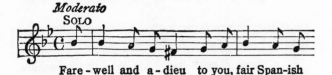

Fare - well and a - dieu to you, fair Span-ish

la - dies, Fare-well and a - dieu to you,

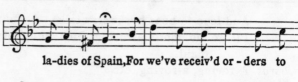

la-dies of Spain, For we've receiv'd or - ders to

sail for old Eng-land; But hope in a short time to

CHORUS

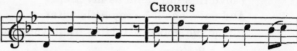

see you a - gain. We'll rant and we'll rove all

o'er the wild o-cean, We'll rant and we'll rove all

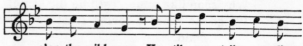

o'er the wild seas, Un - til we strike soundings

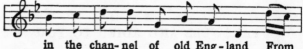

in the chan - nel of old Eng - land From

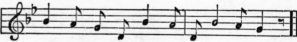

U-shant to Scil - ly is thir - ty-four leagues.

Solo   We hove our ship to, with the wind at
         sou'-west, boys,
           We hove our ship to for to strike sound-
            ings clear;

Then filled the main topsail and bore right
away, boys,
And straight up the Channel our course
we did steer.

Chorus   We'll rant and we'll rove, etc.

Solo   The first land we made was a point called
the Deadman,
Next Ram's Head off Plymouth, Start,
Portland, and Wight;
We sailed then by Beachy, by Fairlee and
Dung'ness,
Then bore straight away for the South
Foreland light.

Chorus   We'll rant and we'll rove, etc.

Solo   The signal was made for the grand fleet to
anchor,
We clewed up our topsails, stuck out
tacks and sheets;
We stood by our stoppers, we brailed in
our spanker,
And anchored ahead of the noblest of
fleets.

Chorus   We'll rant and we'll rove, etc.

Solo   Then let every man here toss off a full
bumper,
Then let every man here toss off his full
bowl,
For we will be jolly and drown melancholy,
With a health to each jovial and true-
hearted soul.

Chorus   We'll rant and we'll rove, etc.

ROLLING HOME

With spirit

Call all hands to man the cap-stan,

See the ca - ble run down clear, Heave a -

way, and with a will, boys, For old

Eng - land we will steer; And we'll

sing in joy - ful cho - rus In the

watch-es of the night, And we'll sight the shores of

Eng-land When the gray dawn brings the light.

Roll - ing home, roll - ing home, roll - ing

home a-cross the sea; Roll-ing home to dear old

Eng-land, Roll-ing home, dear land, to thee.

Solo   Up aloft amid the rigging,
        Blows the loud exulting gale,
        Like a bird's wide out-stretched pinions
        Spreads on high each swelling sail;
        And the wild waves cleft behind us,
        Seem to murmur as they flow,
        There are loving hearts that wait you
        In the land to which you go.

Chorus   Rolling home, etc.

Solo   Many thousand miles behind us,
        Many thousand miles before,
        Ancient ocean heaves to waft us
        To the well-remembered shore.
        Cheer up, Jack, bright smiles await you
        From the fairest of the fair,
        And her loving eyes will greet you
        With kind welcomes everywhere.

Chorus   Rolling home, etc.

HIGH BARBAREE

Quietly

There were two loft - y ships   from

old   Eng - land came, Blow high, . . blow

low, . and so . . sail'd we! One

was   the *Prince of   Lu - ther,* and the

oth - er *Prince of Wales,* Cruising down along the

coast   of the High Bar - bar - ee. . .

"Aloft there, aloft!" our jolly boatswain cries,
    Blow high, blow low, and so sailed we!
"Look ahead, look astern, look a-weather and a-lee,
    Look along down the coast of the High Barbaree."

"There's nought upon the stern, there's nought
   upon the lee,"
   Blow high, blow low, and so sailed we!
"But there's a lofty ship to windward, and she's
   sailing fast and free,
   Sailing down along the coast of the High Bar-
   baree."

"O hail her, O hail her," our gallant captain cried,
   Blow high, blow low, and so sailed we!
"Are you a man-o'-war or a privateer," said he,
   "Cruising down along the coast of the High
   Barbaree?"

"Oh, I am not a man-o'-war nor privateer," said he,
   Blow high, blow low, and so sailed we!
"But I'm a salt-sea pirate a-looking for me fee,
   Cruising down along the coast of the High
   Barbaree."

Oh, 'twas broadside to broadside a long time we
   lay,
   Blow high, blow low, and so sailed we!
Until the Prince of Luther shot the pirate's masts
   away,
   Cruising down along the coast of the High
   Barbaree.

"O quarter, O quarter," those pirates then did cry,
   Blow high, blow low, and so sailed we!
But the quarter that we gave them — we sunk
   them in the sea,
   Cruising down along the coast of the High
   Barbaree.

*THE GOLDEN VANITY

SOLO

There once was a man who was boasting on the quay,

"Oh,   I . . have   a   ship,   and a

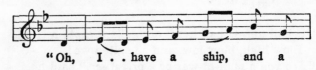

gal-lant ship is she, Of all the ships I know,

she   is   far   the best   to   me, And she's

CHORUS

sailing in the Lowlands low." Lowlands, Lowlands,

She's sail-ing in   the Low-lands low.

Solo   "For I had her built in the North-a-Coun-
tree,
And I had her christened the 'Golden
Vanity':

* The "Golden Vanity" was a once famous ship.

I armed her, and I manned her, and sent
her off to sea
And she's sailing in the Lowlands low."

Chorus Lowlands, Lowlands,
She's sailing in the Lowlands low.

Solo Then up spake a sailor, who'd just re-
turned from sea,
"Oh I was aboard of the 'Golden Vanity';
When she was held in chase by a Spanish
piratee,
And we sank her in the Lowlands low."

Chorus Lowlands, Lowlands,
We sank her in the Lowlands low.

Solo For we had aboard us a little cabin boy,
Who said, "What will you give me if that
ship I do destroy?"
The skipper said, "I'll give my child, she is
my pride and joy,
If you sink her in the Lowlands low."

Chorus Lowlands, Lowlands,
You sink her in the Lowlands low.

Solo The boy took an auger and plunged into
the tide,
And bravely swam until he reached the
rascal pirate's side:
He climbed on board and went below, by
none was he espied, —
And he sank her in the Lowlands low.

Chorus Lowlands, Lowlands,
He sank her in the Lowlands low.

Solo   For he took his auger and let the water
through,
And sank the Spanish pirate craft and all
her rascal crew;
He swam back to the "Vanity," 'twas all
that he could do,
He was sinking in the Lowlands low.

Chorus Lowlands, Lowlands,
Was sinking in the Lowlands low.

Solo   "I'll not take you up now," our cruel cap-
tain cried,
"I'll kill you if you come on deck, to claim
my child as bride —
I'll throw you in the water, I'll drown you
in the tide,
I will sink you in the Lowlands low."

Chorus Lowlands, Lowlands,
Will sink you in the Lowlands low.

Solo   So we took him up, but when on the deck
he died,
We lifted him so tenderly, and sewed him
in a hide;
We said a short prayer o'er him, and
dropped him in the tide,
And he's sailing in the Lowlands low.

Chorus Lowlands, Lowlands,
He's sailing in the Lowlands low.

L'ENVOI

No use to growl, though I sometimes do,
No use to curse that the seas aren't blue —
  And it's hard, black sailing.
To laugh on her icy ropes is best,
To cheer at the wind from the howling West
  And stand to her broken railing.

It's flying-fishmen for a trade-wind sea —
But I'll ask that the guts be granted me
  For the black storm's blowing.
And when I sail, as I some day shall,
To a sailor's unflowered funeral,
  To sing as I'm seaward going.

Bill Adams

INDEX OF AUTHORS

70
71
72
74
76
77
79
83
85